"CHINA JIM"

# WAR AND ITS ALLEGED BENEFITS

By J. NOVIKOW

Vice-President of the International Institute of Sociology.

With a Preface by NORMAN ANGELL
Author of "The Great Illusion"

In one volume, cr. 8vo, price 2s 6d net.

"The book ought to be distributed all over the modern world of armaments and 'great illusions'."—*Daily Mirror*.

LONDON: WILLIAM HEINEMANN.

*James T. Harris*

# "CHINA JIM"
## BEING INCIDENTS AND ADVENTURES IN THE LIFE OF AN INDIAN MUTINY VETERAN

BY

MAJOR-GENERAL J. T. HARRIS

WITH PORTRAIT

The Naval & Military Press Ltd

in association with

The National Army Museum, London

*Published jointly by*

**The Naval & Military Press Ltd**
Unit 10 Ridgewood Industrial Park,
Uckfield, East Sussex,
TN22 5QE England

Tel: +44 (0) 1825 749494
Fax: +44 (0) 1825 765701

www.naval-military-press.com
www.military-genealogy.com
www.militarymaproom.com

*and*

**The National Army Museum, London**
www.national-army-museum.ac.uk

*In reprinting in facsimile from the original, any imperfections are inevitably reproduced and the quality may fall short of modern type and cartographic standards.*

TO
MY DEAR WIFE ELIZABETH
I DEDICATE THIS
BOOK

# FOREWORD

THIS book is not intended in any way to represent History. So many excellent and detailed accounts have been written of the Indian Mutiny by Lord Roberts and others, and of the China Campaign by Lord Wolseley, &c., that I feel it would ill become me, even if I were able, to enter into any sort of competition with such well-known authorities and authors. On the contrary, all that I have set down in these pages is a true account of such episodes and events as have come within my own personal experience, and this only at the oft-repeated request of my many friends and acquaintances.

With reference to the name " China Jim "—after my return from China, in 1861, I found myself constantly addressed and spoken of by this sobriquet; possibly because I got more valuable " loot " from the Summer Palace than any other man in the force. Moreover, the amount that I did get was very much exaggerated, so that I was erroneously supposed by many of my friends to have

# FOREWORD

made an enormous fortune. Hence the title of this book.

I am getting on in life and shall be eighty years of age in May next, and it has given me a certain amount of pleasure and occupation to put down for those who are interested what may seem to others a somewhat egotistical record. Yet I venture to think that we are all more or less egotists at heart. But in the Great Human Family there are always some who respond in harmony to our little note of humour, sentiment, pathos, love of adventure, or what not—and to such I appeal.

J. H.

# CONTENTS

## CHAPTER I

My youth : Voyage to India : Learning to ride : Stannus Fraser and my pony Mutton : Bannatyne Macleod : To Rangoon on a transport : Cockroaches : In charge of the Government elephants at Po-dongmew : We start for Mindoon : A very reticent tiger   Pp. 1–14

## CHAPTER II

The taking of Mindoon : A curious fish : Fever and ague : A trip to Rangoon : MacDowall's treatment for a recalcitrant woman : Invalided home : A generous offer from an American   Pp. 15–22

## CHAPTER III

I return to India : Rumours of the Mutiny : We march to Umballa : Our march to Delhi : Want of sleep : Anger of the Europeans : My first action and sensations during it : Flagstaff Tower : We take the Ridge : Chichester and I go to inspect a battery   Pp. 23–33

## CHAPTER IV

On the Ridge : A narrow shave : Cowards : Another near shave : Reinforcing Hindoo Rao's picket : Utter exhaustion   Pp. 34–39

## CHAPTER V

Despondency and its cure : Defending the vegetable market : Wounded : My attempt to reach Rao's picket : A dangerous position : An invalid : A trying journey : Nerves : In a patent apparatus   Pp. 40–49

# CONTENTS

## CHAPTER VI

An expedition through the hill States : Frost-bite and snow-blindness : An avalanche : For once I get the better of Lord William Hay               Pp. 50–56

## CHAPTER VII

Young "bloods" : A risky ride : Ill-feeling : I win some money and lose it again               Pp. 57–61

## CHAPTER VIII

Digging for treasure in Delhi : Prize auctions : I gain some valuable knowledge : The old King and his habits : On leave : Richard Shebbeare : I join the 15th Punjabees : Our journey to Lucknow : Examinations : The Nana and a letter to W. H. Fitchett               Pp. 62–71

## CHAPTER IX

Faizabad : The Fakir and his powers : Back to Lucknow : Ordered to China : Irritating delays : A quick steamer : Lively times at Singapore : Arrival in China : A sharp but brief dispute : Wolseley : In clover : Feats of strength : Oysters               Pp. 72–81

## CHAPTER X

Peh-tang : A comfortable rut : The Government pawn-broking establishment : Mud : We take the Taku Forts               Pp. 82–87

## CHAPTER XI

On the way to Pekin : The French General in danger : The punishment that failed : My first experience of looting : Tientsin : Capture of guns : Treating for peace : Treachery : Attacking the enemy : A clump of Tartars : A slap in the face : My report and its fate               Pp. 88–100

# CONTENTS

## CHAPTER XII
Peace and prisoners : The shops of Pekin : A French officer and his loot : A wonderful watch : Bargaining with the Frenchman : Pearls of small and great price　　　　　　　　　　　　　　　Pp. 101–110

## CHAPTER XIII
On a looting expedition : Another watch : Baskets of loot : The prize fund : Burning the palace : Gold, and my way of securing it　　　　　　　　　111–121

## CHAPTER XIV
I return to the palace and get more loot : Edmund Ward's story : A piece of bad luck　　Pp. 122–127

## CHAPTER XV
Our march back to Tientsin : Gunboats and language : A terrific gale : An unsuccessful attempt to attract pirates : Turtle-fishing　　　　　　Pp. 128–134

## CHAPTER XVI
Long leave : My marriage and honeymoon : An amusing landlord : Roulette at Baden-Baden : My luck : The Brazilian : Homburg : Married life : Reorganisation of the Indian Army : We go to Calcutta　　Pp. 135–144

## CHAPTER XVII
An unsatisfactory interview : A swindle : Kindness of the Viceroy : More interviews : Barrackpore : The great cyclone　　　　　　　　　　Pp. 145–154

## CHAPTER XVIII
At Dorunda : G. : March to Ferozepore : Quarrels and plain speaking : I am put under arrest : But in spite of this am appointed Acting Magistrate : I offer to go to Abyssinia : Moradabad　　　　　　Pp. 155–162

# CONTENTS

## CHAPTER XIX

Butterfly : The Meerut Tent Club : A chronicle : A picnic worth remembering          Pp. 163-171

## CHAPTER XX

Simla : We go to Morar, Gwalior : Success of Butterfly : Colonel Gowan : We go home : An experience : Back to India : The favourite beaten : Lord Mayo   Pp. 172-180

## CHAPTER XXI

The same old errand : I have my eyes opened : Interview with Lord Napier : Am offered a command : Lord Napier's experience of the Gwalas : We go to Delhi : A parade : I explain my views to my officers          Pp. 181-191

## CHAPTER XXII

Improvement of the regiment : An inspection : Praise and explanations : A good dinner : Snakes : Sham fights : The Prince of Wales's visit : A new game of tennis : Ulwar : A magnificent picnic   Pp. 192-209

## CHAPTER XXIII

Native history : Exploration : Buried treasure : A company is formed : Difficulties with the directors : Farewell          Pp. 210-218

# CHAPTER I

My Youth : Voyage to India : Learning to Ride : Stannus Fraser and my pony Mutton : Bannatyne Macleod : To Rangoon on a Transport : Cockroaches : In charge of the Government Elephants at Podongmew : We start for Mindoon : A very reticent Tiger

WHEN anyone begins to write his reminiscences he is, at the outset, faced with a difficulty. If he mentions his early days he is in danger of boring his readers, and if he does not mention them he may be accused of omitting something which I hope I may be excused for calling vital. I will endeavour to overcome this difficulty by being as brief as possible.

I was born at Coundon, in Warwickshire, in 1832. My mother was the daughter of Sir Lachlan Maclean and my father's people were bankers. Therefore, when questioned by curious persons about my ancestors, I have usually told them that I am descended partly from cattle-stealers and partly from bankers.

I was sent to a very good private school in the village of Allesley, Warwickshire, and at the age of seventeen I was given an Indian cadetship by Sir John Cam Hobhouse, then President of the Board of Control. The

## REMINISCENCES OF

date of this was June 27, 1849, and on the same date the good ship *Barham*, one of Green's Indiamen, left the Thames.

I joined the *Barham* at Spithead on July 1. The voyage was a long one, and full of, what were to me, interesting incidents. But in these days it seems to me that one may be very sure of two things, firstly that many people who take voyages will write about them, and secondly that what they may write has to be extraordinarily far from the commonplace if it is to be received with any pretence of welcome. Interesting, then, as this voyage was to me in my boyhood, I cannot imagine that it would have the smallest interest to anyone at the present time.

We touched at Madras, and landed in Calcutta on October 15. My age was seventeen and a half, and I did not know a single soul in India. Without delay I reported myself to the superintendent of cadets, and was given quarters in Fort William. The East India Company treated their cadets excellently, and I found both a capital mess and very comfortable quarters. There I waited for a couple of months, until I got my orders to join the 57th Native Infantry at Dinapur.

I confess that I did not like the 57th

## THE INDIAN MUTINY

when I joined them. But presently they were ordered away and I was posted to the 67th in the same station; they proved to be a much nicer set of fellows. After two or three months I found myself posted to the 2nd European Bengal Fusiliers, one of the old Company's famous European regiments.

I was to join at Agra, and, as there were no railways at that time in India, I went by river steamer to Allahabad and thence by dāk-gharrie to Agra. My regiment marched in on March 2, 1850, and at once I found myself at home. In those days a regiment was one's home, for means of communication being conspicuous by their absence, nobody ever thought of leave. Every night of our lives between thirty and forty of us used to sit down to mess, and we were a convivial and happy family party.

Within a few months I got a sharp attack of small-pox, and when recovering was offered six months' leave to the Himalayas, but I refused to go. The regiment was my home, and the rest of India had little charm for me. Nowadays it is a very different thing, for everyone who can get leave in the hot weather is only too glad to take it.

Game was plentiful and I learnt to shoot, and also to ride. I bought my first pony from the postmaster at Allahabad, and I doubt if anyone has ever learnt to ride in a more gyratory school than mine. My animal was what is called "a character," for he was very amusing and exceedingly vicious. His chief aim in life was to throw me off, and in this he succeeded about twice a day for over a year. But, having, so to speak, "done his job," he was obviously quite satisfied and always waited for me to remount. On the whole I am inclined to think that he must have enjoyed himself more than I did.

The consequence of often being picked up at the corners of roads in the cantonment was that my brother officers came to the —perhaps natural—conclusion that I was useless as a horseman. One day at mess, however, we happened to be talking about riding, when Stannus Fraser jeered at me, and said that my opinion on the matter was not worth listening to.

This annoyed me, so I said, "At any rate I will bet you can't ride my pony, Mutton, at a canter past my gate without being taken in, and I'll bet you five gold mohurs that I can."

Now Fraser was about the smartest young fellow in the regiment, a thoroughly good-all-round man, and he immediately took my bet.

## THE INDIAN MUTINY

Everybody came out to see the fun, and I, knowing my pony by this time, rode past the gate without the slightest difficulty. Then Fraser mounted a hundred yards down the main road, and going off rather smartly was carried through the gate and right up to the house at the rate of forty miles an hour. He hurt his knee very badly against the gate, and he also lost five gold mohurs.

Afterwards I got the knack of picking up stones in the road at full gallop off this pony, and could even throw my whip ahead and pick it up again. Indeed I do not think that I was ever thrown again by Mutton, for he, possibly, was tired of his amusements and I was certainly a better horseman.

About this time I was fortunate enough to make a most sincere and true friend. His name was Bannatyne Macleod, and he was Superintending Surgeon of Agra, a rank which corresponds to the present Deputy Inspector-General of Hospitals. He insisted that I should go to live with him, and he obtained my colonel's permission for me to do so.

For about two years I lived with him in the most intimate companionship. He was a free-thinker, a very clever man, and held what were then, at least, considered to be very peculiar notions about the next world.

Often he declared that if it should be possible for him to communicate with me after death, he would most assuredly do so. I mention this now because later on I shall have something more to say upon the subject.

Life at Agra was most pleasant, but after staying there for over two years we were ordered to Calcutta, and proceeded there by native boats down the Jumna and Ganges. There we remained until, in the autumn of '52, we were ordered to Rangoon.

The way the Government, in those days, looked upon the European soldiers' accommodation was very different from what it is now. Some four companies of my regiment were placed on board a transport, called the *Kenilworth*, of about 400 tons. Now this vessel had been employed to carry sugar from Mauritius to Calcutta, and was consequently full of every imaginable sort of insect life.

Each officer was given a cabin to himself, but when I put my head into mine I was fairly and squarely defeated by the smell, and promptly made it over to my native servants, who held possession all the way to Rangoon. As the weather was very fine I slept on deck during the first night, and woke up about 2 A.M. feeling rather uneasy. At that time I always used oil on my hair

# THE INDIAN MUTINY

for the sake of coolness, and when I put my hands to my head I found that my hair was positively swarming with cockroaches which were busily engaged in eating the oil. From this occupation I speedily disturbed them, and then found that all my toe-nails had been eaten to the quick.

At dawn I got hold of the first mate, and suggested that the cause, or one of the causes, of this excess of cockroaches was that the rudder post of the ship came up through a well to the poop; and on looking carefully down this well we saw thousands and thousands of cockroaches. We then proceeded to fill all the fire-buckets in the ship and a lot of the men's grog-tubs with sea-water and, at a given moment, dashed them all into the well; this we continued to do until no cockroach was to be seen.

My chief recollections of the *Kenilworth* are connected with insects, for in addition to those against which I made such a determined attack, we were also accompanied by myriads of sugar ants. These are minute red insects, much smaller than a pin's head, and the men, who had the whole of the hold as quarters, suffered tremendously from their superfluous attentions.

Shortly after reaching Rangoon we were ordered up to Prome, where we spent the hot weather. My regiment went to Burmah 1100 strong, but by the end of that year we had lost 500 men and five officers. Every man, from the colonel downwards, had fever and ague every other day, in addition to most of the cutaneous diseases to which our flesh is heir.

Before the hot weather set in, however, I was sent to an out-station, sixteen miles below Prome on the right bank of the Irrawaddy, called Po-dongmew. There I had a delightful time, for very soon I found myself commanding the station and the only European officer present.

An extraordinary epidemic had attacked the Government elephants, and Po-dongmew, having an abundance of fodder, was considered to be the most healthy place for them. Consequently I found myself in charge of 437 elephants, and was delighted to have such a novel experience. I was constantly in their keddah, rode one or two daily, and became very friendly with some of them. But there was one point about these elephants that did not please me, and this I mentioned to the Jemadar.

"You natives," I said to him, "think a great deal about the completeness of the hairs of the elephant's tails. But you seem to have a very bad lot here, and any number of

# THE INDIAN MUTINY

elephants have lost their tails altogether. How do you explain this?"

"I will show you, Sahib," he replied, and took me up to a remarkable-looking elephant with a very red eye.

I did not fancy this animal in the very least, but on being assured that he was quite harmless to Europeans, I went up and took hold of his trunk and talked to him.

"That elephant," the Jemadar continued, "is the cause of all the trouble. He would never hurt a man, but he is mad to bite off the tails of other elephants."

Two days after I heard a tremendous noise in the keddah, and rushing out of my tent I saw this elephant, with his trunk curled in the air, coming along at a tearing speed and carrying another elephant's tail in his mouth.

I got to know a great many of these elephants, and to watch their ways was a most interesting study. Often I used to take out as many as a hundred at a time, and having formed them in line we beat down the grass jungles in the neighbourhood. On these occasions I myself drove a female elephant, called Lutchnee—the pleasantest animal I ever knew. In those days I had only a small-bore gun, and I am bound to confess that game was as plentiful as my bags were small.

The Burmese War was now over, and our frontier with Upper Burmah had been defined on the map as 19 deg. 20 min. Thus it became necessary, in the midst of the jungles, to discover where 19 deg. 20 min. was. And this was especially indispensable, as there was said to be a town called Mindoon, and nobody knew whether it was on our side of the boundary or on the Upper Burmah side; for, it must be remembered, we had only annexed Lower Burmah.

Soon afterwards I heard that the Chief Commissioner, Colonel A. Phayre, was coming to Po-dongmew, and thence was going to start with a force to discover the town of Mindoon. The force was to consist of fifty Europeans of my regiment and a hundred natives of the 65th Bengal Infantry, and for carriage we were to rely upon elephants.

The country from Po-dongmew up to the frontier was supposed to reach over nearly 150 miles, and to be thickly wooded and with no suspicion of a road. This supposition proved to be perfectly correct, and in some places we found the jungle to be so thick that we could not advance more than half a mile in a day. In other places, where there had been jungle fires, we managed to get on more quickly.

# THE INDIAN MUTINY

To me this was a most delightful journey, for it was impossible to tell what one might see or meet. The country was quite uninhabited, although we certainly did come across one man. He had a fire and a sumpitan—that is, a hollow blow-pipe about six feet long. This old man of the jungle got his living by shooting small birds (mostly partridges) with little darts through this tube. In answer to our questions he replied that he "sought and found," a peculiarly terse way of summing up his existence.

I was constantly with the advance guard, which consisted of a corporal and four men. When we came out into an open bit of jungle, the black partridge, usually a most shy bird, would come up to me as I rode on my pony, and run along by the side of my stirrup. The bird used to look at me inquisitively, as much as to say, "What sort of strange animal are you?" Nearly every time that we pitched camp we caught several hares, and sometimes even birds.

One day, just as we were pitching our tents, two sambhur with a young hind behind them came close to us. The sambhur cleared their way, but the hind stumbled over an elephant's coolie, with the result that we had venison for dinner. I do not know what game-hunters of the present day would think of twenty men falling on the top of a hind, but that was the way in which we secured our venison.

Later on, when we were in a ravine country covered with bamboo jungle, I borrowed a coolie from the hospital, and went out to see if I could shoot a few jungle fowl. The only way one could walk in this country was along the bottom of the ravines, which were full of dry leaves of bamboo. After I had got some five miles from camp, and had shot three jungle cocks, I came to an insuperable bunker in the form of a dense thorn jungle. There I sat down, for as I was compelled to go back along the same ravine by which I had come, I thought that I would wait for an hour or so in the hope that some of the game I had disturbed might return.

I had proceeded for about a mile on my homeward journey, when I saw a large tiger, apparently fast asleep, and with his tail-end towards me, lying comfortably along the bottom of the ravine. Now, to get back to the camp, I had to walk over the very spot where he was, so I dropped a bullet down over my small shot into one barrel, and for a second bullet, which had been carried in my mouth and had got a little bitten, I had to use a ramrod. This made a noise, and the tiger raised his head. Then he licked his shoulder, and looked along his body at me just as a cat might have looked.

When I had pointed out the tiger to Dabee Deen, my coolie, he remarked, " Yes, Sahib, you will kill him now that you have put down the bullets." On this point I did not feel anything like so confident as the coolie appeared to be ; but as the difficulty had to be faced, I went round a little bend of the ravine to within a few yards of him. Then the tiger got up, stretched himself, and snarled.

His next move was to look at me with what I considered a rather morbid interest. I returned his stare. I had made up my mind not to fire until he crouched to spring, when I hoped to give him one in the eye, and to jump aside as he sprang ; and subsequently, if possible, to give him the other bullet as he passed by. So much for my programme, but the tiger would not assist me to carry it out.

Presently he began to walk slowly away, and I walked after him. When he stopped I pretended to be admiring the scenery. When he walked on I followed. In this way we proceeded for over a quarter of a mile, when he strolled up one side of the ravine into the deep jungle, leaving me in the ticklish position of having to pass, with my gun ready, under the spot where he had just disappeared ; but I never saw him again. Possibly the reasons for his reticent behaviour were that I was the first man he had ever seen, and that he did not happen to be hungry.

# CHAPTER II

The taking of Mindoon : A curious fish : Fever and ague : A trip to Rangoon : MacDowall's treatment for a recalcitrant woman : Invalided home : A generous offer from an American

WE wandered through this beautiful country for thirty days or more, and then the native scouts reported that we were approaching Mindoon. At the moment we were on the banks of a beautiful and very clear river, which must have its source in the Arracan Hills. We also began to see signs of a path, and evidently were returning to the habitations of men.

During dinner on that night Colonel Phayre said that he would like somebody to go on and reconnoitre, and I at once volunteered. The Commanding Officer gave me one duffadar and eight sowars, who were also a part of our force; and I was accompanied by two Burmese headmen, each of whom had a servant or friend, and an interpreter, thus making fifteen men, all mounted. In addition I was given twenty men of the 65th Native Infantry, who had been picked for fast walking.

At 2 A.M. on that same night we started along the faint signs of a path, and by the earliest dawn we found ourselves about 400 yards from the gates of Mindoon. On inspection, Mindoon turned out to be a strongly stockaded place. It was surrounded almost entirely by the river, and a deep moat had been cut round the only open place, so that it was practically an island. From the spot on which we had halted I could see two very narrow bamboo bridges across the moat, and these led to the big gateway.

We waited until the gates had been opened and then we rode at full gallop, the duffadar making for one bridge and I for the other. We succeeded in getting to the gate before it could be closed, and almost everyone ran away as we arrived. The town seemed to be full of people, the majority of whom were women. I immediately took possession of a large white temple, which was covered with highly coloured paintings on a white ground of the tortures of the Burmese hell. It was not the kind of place which lent itself to any undue exaltation of spirits, and I was very glad when, a few hours later, I saw the remainder of the force marching in.

Mindoon itself was extremely beautiful, and its river so attractive to a fisherman that, having a fish-hook with some line in an old pocket-book, I determined to try my luck. Having got a tapering bamboo from the

## THE INDIAN MUTINY

jungle, I put a common house-fly on the hook and soon caught a fish exactly like an English dace.

Seeing, however, bigger fellows than this one swimming about, I put on a worm and dropped it into a nice pool, in which there were half a dozen big fish, but of a most peculiar colour. Presently I caught one and hauled him out, a proceeding which he resented in a manner entirely novel—and not excessively amusing—to me. As a matter of fact, he blew himself into a round ball, nearly as big as a football, and barked at me so ferociously that I had no wish to have anything more to do with him. If he was not poisonous his appearance was exceptionally deceptive.

We stayed at Mindoon for about ten days, and all of us were very sorry to leave it. The town was famous for a particular kind of tobacco, which was said to be the best in Burmah, and that, indeed, seemed to be the only cultivation around the place.

From there we marched to Thayetmyo, on the Irrawaddy, but the only remarkable things about Thayetmyo were the complete absence of sanitary arrangements and the extraordinary number of fleas. The ground on which we encamped was a whitish sand, but until you began to put a foot down it was black with fleas, and it became white as you walked.

From Thayetmyo I went down the river by steamer and rejoined the regiment at Prome, and from that time disease, mostly fever and ague, set in. So virulent did it become that the Government ordered the formation of a new station on a large promontory which jutted out into the Irrawaddy. This place was called Namyan, and there wooden barracks were erected and we officers received orders to build our own houses. In fact we were refused leave until we had, at least, begun to build.

I was really rather pleased with my first attempt to build a house of wood and bamboo; but by the time it was nearly ready for a house-warming this new station had become so terribly unhealthy that of the two hundred men and officers in occupation of it, there were only a very few who could walk to the steamer which was sent to take us off.

Two other outpost stations were formed at Upper and Lower Showedoung, where we were quartered in poongy houses and temples, and these stations were certainly healthier. Unable, however, to get free of fever, I was recommended to take a trip down to Rangoon and back again by the river steamer.

# THE INDIAN MUTINY

At Rangoon I stayed with Charlie Mac-Dowall, who related to me an experience of his which, in these days of militant and law-breaking women, I cannot refrain from putting down.

One evening I had started the conversation with an account of my taking the town of Mindoon—up to that time my only independent command.

"Ah," Mac said, "it's all very well commanding men, but it is quite another thing to be in charge of women on the line of march. If a woman gets drunk, what can you do? There is no prison, and you can't handcuff her and make her march tied to a cart as you would a man."

I assured him that I could think of nothing to meet the case, and he continued: "When I brought down the regimental depôt from the hills to Agra after the Punjab campaign, I had about fifty women, a lot of children, and a dozen or so of more or less weakly men. But fortunately I had Colour-Sergeant James Monks with me, and what I should have done without him I don't know. When we left Kalka nearly everyone was drunk, and Monks and I found that the women had been selling liquor to the men. Things went from bad to worse, and though we could keep the men from getting liquor for themselves, we could not prevent the women from selling it to them. The worst offender was a big Irishwoman whose name began with an M, and when she was sober Monks brought her before me under a guard."

The recollection of this violent lady caused MacDowall to pause for an instant, but I urged him to tell me how he had dealt with her.

"She would not listen to anything I had to say," he told me, "but her stock of bad language was the largest I have ever listened to. Now, I had been consulting with Monks and he had recommended two courses. The first I put into practice then and there. Calling for the regimental water-carriers, we made Mrs. M. sit down while they thoroughly soused her with water. Perhaps this treatment quieted her a little, but the flow of water didn't do much to stop her flow of language. Two or three days afterwards she was again before me for the same offence, and once more we were all most vilely abused."

"However," continued MacDowall, "Monks and I had still another card up our sleeves. 'Mrs. M.,' I said, 'I could not have believed that any woman could so disgrace her sex. I must try a new form of punishment.' Turning to the sergeant, I said,

## THE INDIAN MUTINY

'Monks, send for the regimental barber.' When the barber had come I ordered him to cut off Mrs. M.'s hair until only about half an inch of it was left all round her head.

"'Yu'll never do it. Shure ye wouldn't do such a thing,' she exclaimed.

"'There's nothing else I can do,' I said, 'and at any rate that is the punishment you are to receive.'

"Then she went down on her knees and called upon the Holy Virgin to protect her, and swore that she would never sell a drop of liquor again, and went on to beg my pardon and to say what a 'dear, good, kind man' I was.

"'Well,' I said, 'you shall be forgiven this time, but remember the next time your conduct is outrageous off your hair comes.'

"She went away to her tent and we never had any more trouble with her, and I've never given up thanking Monks for proposing such an effective punishment."

"After all," I said to MacDowall when he had finished, "it is only giving women the same treatment as men."

And to this day it seems to me that if women commit wanton outrages, they ought to be punished in an efficacious way.

At Rangoon I was attended by an assistant surgeon, named White, who said that I ought

# REMINISCENCES

to be sent to England, and so I was invalided home and left Calcutta early in April in the P. & O. steamer *Bentinck*. At Point-de-Galle several Americans came on board, and began to play poker every afternoon.

I thought that I should like to learn the game, for, although I had never played it before, I had played a good deal at "brag," and thought that the latter game was very much like poker. In a very few days nearly all the players owed me money, and before we landed I had won a considerable stake.

On board there was a most agreeable American. He had just resigned the Consulship of the Sandwich Islands, and was one of the best fellows I have ever met. He was very kind to me, and before we got to Suez he said, "Look here, Harris, I would like you to go all over Europe with me, and apart from wanting to see Rome and Venice I don't care a bit where I go. You shall be with me for six months, and I'll pay all expenses and take you through England and to my home in America." The generosity of this offer cannot be denied, and I have often thought how silly I was to refuse it, but the fact was I was very anxious to get home and see my mother.

# CHAPTER III

I return to India : Rumours of the Mutiny : We march to Umballa : Our march to Delhi : Want of sleep : Anger of the Europeans : My first action and sensations during it : Flagstaff Tower : We take the Ridge : Chichester and I go to inspect a Battery

I STAYED in England for eighteen months and lived mostly in rooms in Jermyn Street. Of course I fell in love, and with my first love to whom I had been attached ever since she was thirteen. I could not, however, afford to marry, so I left England in the autumn of '56, and after making a trip through Spain I joined the P. *&* O. steamer at Gibraltar.

Having arrived at Calcutta, I reported myself at the Adjutant-General's office and then went to see Dan O'Callaghan, who was garrison surgeon of Fort William and a man famous for his tiffins. I stayed to tiffin, and Dan asked me what I was going to do. In reply I said that I should go up and stay with Bannatyne Macleod at Umballa—to which place I knew that Macleod had been transferred, because we had written to each other by every mail since we had parted four years before.

"Oh," O'Callaghan said, "then you have not heard?"

"I am only just off ship, and have heard nothing," I answered.

Whereupon O'Callaghan told me that Bannatyne was dead, and I knew then that he was unable to communicate with me; for had he been able, I felt quite satisfied, in my own mind, that he would have done so.

Being allowed—under the Bengal regulations of the H.E.I.C.—marching time to join my regiment, I was not compelled to hurry, and so I had plenty of opportunity to amuse myself on the way up to Umballa.

At that time there was only one railway (of 121 miles) in India, which went to Raniganj and the Bengal coal-fields. From Raniganj I had to go by dāk-gharrie up to Allahabad and thence to Cawnpore, where the other battalion of my regiment, the 1st European Bengal Fusiliers, was then stationed. I had a very pleasant time, and again met the Nana, whose acquaintance I had first made in 1851-52. Afterwards I stayed at Lucknow and Agra, and passing through Delhi I, at length, rejoined my regiment at Umballa towards the end of March.

No idea of the impending mutiny had entered my mind, but in Umballa it became evident that the country was very much disturbed. The firing of bungalows was rife, and the attitude of the sepoys was by

## THE INDIAN MUTINY

no means what it had been. But we in the European regiment were not in the least anxious about this.

In the early part of April we marched up to Subathoo, which was our proper station. The first battalion marched up from Cawnpore to Dagshai, and the 75th, now the Gordon Highlanders, marched to Kussoulie, all three of these stations being in the lower hills.

About May 1 I got ten days' leave to Simla, where I stayed with Lord William Hay; and as I rode down to rejoin at Subathoo I received the first news of the mutiny from W. Plowden, B.C.S. I met him riding a tired pony close to the Hurreepore Bridge, and he asked me to exchange my pony for his. But when he told me of the mutiny at Meerut, and of the massacre of women and children, I said that I expected we should march down on the following day, and that I should want my pony.

My expectations were realised, for next day we got orders to march down to Umballa, but even then we did not believe that the trouble was really serious. I remember, when marching up the hill to Kussoulie, that I was beside the Adjutant-General on the narrow pathway, and asked him if he thought we were really going down to Delhi, for my private opinion was that we should not get farther than Umballa. I was, therefore, very considerably relieved when he replied that we should certainly go down to Delhi, and take it if we could.

In the evening we reached Kussoulie, messed with the 75th, and we slept on the floor of the mess-room. Next morning we were up early, and reached Umballa in two days, making one halt on the way. We marched all night and the next night, for the weather was terribly hot, but the flies prevented us from getting any sleep in the daytime. Ultimately we straggled into Umballa at 9 A.M. The men went into barracks, and the officers, fifty-seven of us in all, were ordered into the unfurnished and unoccupied mess-house of the 14th Foot.

Peake and Allen, the chemists and big store-keepers of Umballa, had just obtained some soda-water machines from England, and they provided us with lemonade, ginger-beer, and other effervescing drinks to which we had hitherto been unaccustomed. Our thirst, I may say, was appalling. From the native bazaar we managed to get a sufficient number of charpoys, and tried to make ourselves as comfortable as possible and to curb our impatience, for naturally we were all

## THE INDIAN MUTINY

full of anxiety to march down to Delhi. Two native regiments were known to be disaffected there, and every thatched bungalow in the place had been burned down by the natives, who had fired burning arrows into the thatch.

Day after day, however, to our increasing disgust and disappointment, we were kept in that old mess-house to wait for the arrival of a siege-train from Philaur. At last, towards the end of the month, this train, consisting of six 18-pounders and six 8-inch howitzers, with some cohorns, arrived, and we marched towards Delhi.

The heat was frightful, and the dust beyond anything I had ever seen in my life. We always started to march at about 6 P.M., and about 9 A.M. we got into a camping ground. As I never could sleep during the day, especially when I wanted to, I shall never forget the tortures I suffered from want of sleep. Marching at about two miles an hour as we were, I used to fall off my pony five or six times every night. When I fell off I thanked God I was off, and there I lay until the rear-guard pulled me to my feet. Then I would march in the ranks between the men, and stagger from one side to the other against my neighbours.

Eventually we reached Raie, which was,

as far as I remember, about eleven miles from Delhi. There a scene occurred which showed the feeling of the Europeans. A Lancer man, after our tents were pitched, rode through the camp with the foot and part of the leg of a small European child, which he had found somewhere on the road. The foot still had a little shoe upon it, and the gruesome spectacle so enraged our troops that in a few minutes twenty natives were hanging on the nearest tree.

At Raie we heard that the mutineers had taken up a position across the Grand Trunk road, about four or five miles farther on, and that they had erected a battery and had some seventy guns in position.

Our artillery, followed by the infantry, moved off at early dawn, and, true to report, we found the enemy strongly posted right across the Grand Trunk road. As we came within range of the guns each regiment deployed into line.

We were on the extreme left, the 75th in the centre opposite to the biggest battery, and the 1st Fusiliers on the right. In front of us there were only two batteries of Horse Artillery, newly turned out from the Arsenal in Delhi. They were so like our own men that several times I gave orders to cease firing, because I thought that we were firing

# THE INDIAN MUTINY

upon our own fellows. The 75th, on our right, stormed the big battery at once, and lost about 70 men; but we had an easier task. We captured most of the Horse Artillery guns, tumbril, and ammunition wagons, and also a large store-cart full of rupees. Then we halted and re-formed line.

Before we went into action I had been extremely nervous as to what my behaviour would be in this my first fight. Let me say, then, that I found it most delightful, and I think I may add that, as long as one is advancing in line against anything in the world, *as long as one can advance*, fighting is a pleasure to the majority of soldiers. I felt very much relieved at my total lack of " nerves," and looked forward to more fighting. The man next to me in my company, a private of the name of Alpin, got a round shot which took off his leg. It did not upset me at all. My pay-sergeant, Donovan, got another round shot which took off his right arm high up at the shoulder, and the arm caught the adjutant, Coghill, right in the face. This incident, which, when remembered in cold blood, is sufficiently horrible, seemed to me at the moment to be very amusing. The place where we had been fighting was called Bad-li-ke-serai.

We were now within three or four miles

from the ridge outside Delhi, and we could see the enemy's artillery on the top of it. Having crossed a small nullah by a bridge, we came out on the Grand Parade, which is exactly where our King George was encamped at the last Durbar. No sooner did we reach this parade-ground than we inclined to the left and made for the Flagstaff road on the ridge. Immediately the guns opened upon our flank. We were in columns of companies, and I discovered to my surprise that I did not like it at all. As we got nearer, and began to climb the rocky ridge, the feeling became worse. Of all sounds in the world, that of grape-shot striking rocks is the most discomforting and disagreeable!

There was a good road up to the Flagstaff Tower on the top of the ridge, and, turning to the right at the top, we soon cleared the enemy's artillery off the ridge. There we came across eight or ten artillery carts, filled with the dried bodies of women and children who had been massacred. On our way down from Umballa we had met various suffering ladies and children, and I must say that the prevailing feeling among us was that we should like to kill every sepoy we saw.

By 9 A.M. we had taken the whole ridge. Pickets were formed at the Flagstaff, the

## THE INDIAN MUTINY

Mosque, the Observatory, and Hindoo Rao's. In the early afternoon the rest of us marched back to the Grand Parade, and I found myself for quarter-guard duty.

Presently Hodson came up to me with the joyful news that he could give me some lunch, and, sitting on the ground, we had it together. I had known both Hodson and his wife very well in Umballa, and during a long varied and eventful life I have never seen a finer cavalry soldier than he was. That lunch is impressed upon my memory. A kitmutghar brought us a meat-pie cooked in a tin pie-dish. The heat had turned everything sour, and of course we had no bread. But we were given chupatties and BEER. I am told that someone has since written a song in praise of beer, but I do not think that anyone can realise what we thought of beer in June '57.

When our tents had been pitched I found that I was in an old hill tent, which had no chiks to speak of. It was during that day, and, indeed, throughout the whole siege, about as full of flies as it could hold. We were all very tired and anxious to get some sleep, but my chief suffering while we were before Delhi always came from want of sleep. Food I could then, and can now, do without, but sleep is a necessity. Being on duty, I remained with the guard during that first night, so that I could be wakened.

On the following day, June 9, I found myself quite fit again, and at noon a great friend of mine, Hugh Chichester, a subaltern of the Royal Artillery, came to my fly-infested tent. He was full of the news that during the night the artillery had erected a battery in front of Hindoo Rao's for an 18-pounder and an 8-inch howitzer, and he wanted me to go up to the ridge with him to see it.

This was great and exciting news, and, perhaps naturally, we imagined that Delhi was going to be taken at once. Neither Chichester nor I had ever seen a real battery, and we had scarcely got into it and had time to think what a small thing it was before every gun in Delhi opened fire upon us— from the Cashmere, the Moree, the Lahore, and other batteries.

Some of these guns were 32-pounders, and in less than a minute two men had their heads taken off by round shot and many others were wounded. Very little cover was to be found, and I sat down between the howitzer and the gun, and kept saying to myself, "Well, to think I came here for pleasure!" I also wondered how on earth I was going to get away. Anyone in search

# THE INDIAN MUTINY

of amusement is strongly advised by me not to try to find it by sitting in a small battery which is being pounded by heavy guns.

Presently, however, the enemy were tired of firing, and I walked slowly away, endeavouring, as I went, to suggest to myself that I was rather enjoying it. One of the limbers, a little further to the rear, was blown up by a shell and eight gunners were blown up with it. Their clothes were alight, and some of them had half of their bodies blown away. All of them were in a terrible state, and some were begging their comrades to bayonet them and put them out of their misery. I think that it is astonishing how very soon one forgets these sights in action, and how small an impression they make at the moment.

From this time I was constantly on picket duty. Delhi was really fought by subalterns. We had only two captains, and one of them was very ill. So short of officers were we that I commanded three companies.

## CHAPTER IV

On the ridge : A narrow shave : Cowards : Another near shave : Reinforcing Hindoo Rao's picket : Utter exhaustion

EVENTUALLY we received reinforcements, but I cannot say precisely when they joined us. I believe the 60th Rifles and the Carbineers from Meerut came in before Badli-ke-serai, but I did not happen to see them. I, however, watched the Guides (who made that famous march from Hotimurdan at an average of twenty-two miles a day) arrive, and not a man had fallen out. From the line of march they went straight into action. It is good to remember those splendid fellows. Nor let me forget the Ghoorkas, under Major Reid, who lived on the ridge during the whole siege, and on the most exposed part of it. They suffered more than any of us, for they were constantly under fire, day and night.

On June 12 I found myself in orders to relieve the picket of the 75th at the Flagstaff Tower. We arrived at earliest dawn, and were at once attacked and our skirmishers driven in. Captain Knox, who commanded the two companies of the 75th, was shot through the head, and the next captain disappeared.

# THE INDIAN MUTINY

Two light guns, under Bishop, R.A., were on the right of the tower, pointing down the road to the Cashmere Gate, and as the skirmishers ran past the guns at the double I remember apologising to Bishop for falling back behind him, and saying, as I went by him, "I must form up these fellows." For they were all in a confused crowd in the rear of a limber, firing in the air, and more or less in a state of panic. The language I used was, I am sure, more powerful than polite, but there was little or nothing for me to do.

My colour-sergeant, Jerry Noon, who was firing in the air as fast as he could load, filled me with such violent fury that I rushed at him, intending to cut him down. But just in time he put up his musket to save himself, and I allowed my sword to come down on his bayonet.

Then I stood out with my back to the enemy in front of the limber and the men, and tried to persuade them to form line and come on. While I was standing in this position I suddenly became aware of a bayonet close to my left ear, and being quick on my feet I jumped backwards and sideways into a hole from which earth had been taken to fill the sandbags in front of the guns.

This was a lucky excavation for me. As I jumped in the Jemadar fired over my shoulder, whereupon I, leaping out, caught him with my regulation sword on the side of his neck. I thought that I had cut his head clean off. The cutting down of the enemy's leader had a tonic effect on my men, and, headed by one Jerry Lynch, they came out from behind the limber. Then some fifty men, under the sergeant-major, came up from the camp and joined us, and without a single stop we drove the enemy down the slope and right up to the walls of Delhi. As we returned to the Flagstaff my attention was drawn to the Jemadar's body, and we found that his head was hanging by a little piece of skin.

After this I generally found myself on the Mosque picket, which was comparatively an easier post because there was some shade from the Minarets. It was two-storied, and the officers lived on the top story. During the day the enemy amused themselves by firing an 8-inch shell at us every five minutes. But they rarely managed to hit us, and as the siege progressed their shooting became decidedly worse, owing no doubt to their best men having been killed.

I have to add that after the affair at the Flagstaff Tower I was so enraged with my

## THE INDIAN MUTINY

men that I went into every one of the tents of my particular company and made a point of calling each man a coward. Some of them, of course, were very indignant. Nevertheless I insisted upon it, because it was true that until I had cut down the Jemadar I had not been able to get any of them to form line or follow me.

I reaped the benefit of this when, a few days later, being on the Mosque picket, I got a sudden order to reinforce Hindoo Rao's picket. Now the road between the Mosque and Hindoo Rao's ran along the top of the ridge, and was very plainly visible from the walls of Delhi.

I marched in column of fours, and, immediately on my left, marched a Sikh belonging to the Guides, to whom I was talking as we walked. Looking back over my shoulder, I saw that my men were beginning to straggle, so I gave the order, " Mark time." The Sikh, however, not being under my orders, continued to march on, and he had advanced about ten paces when the enemy on the Moree bastion fired two guns with shrapnel at us. But for that command, " Mark time," both the leading files and I must have been swept away. As it was the Sikh was unharmed, although the back of his uniform was torn in several places, and the front of mine was also torn. But not a man was hurt.

In fairness to my men it is only right to say here that not only on this occasion but ever afterwards the discipline of my company was to my mind perfect, and there was always between us that mutual trust, difficult to arrive at, but which, when attained, is the most valuable asset that man or officer can possess.

When I resumed the march I took care to get off the road, for I found that it was a foolish trick to be on the sky-line. I think that this day was June 23, and it was certainly the turning-point of the siege.

I never saw men so utterly done up as the whole of the picket was at Hindoo Rao's, for there was hardly a drop of water to be got. The enemy had already made six attacks, and while I was there some officer called out, " Fall in ; the enemy are streaming out of Lahore Gate." Not a man moved in answer to this command. They were sitting and lying about in any scrap of shade they could find, with their tongues black in their mouths. My own men were nearly the only ones fit for service, and I marched on to the right, where the Ghoorkas were, and told Major Reid that my men were ready. At this he expressed

# THE INDIAN MUTINY

great pleasure, and added that he was sure everyone else was too tired and exhausted to fight. The enemy, however, did not attack again, and I saw them retreat back to the Lahore Gate. Had they attacked just once more, they must have driven us off the ridge, for I had only thirty-two men with me, and we had been on picket duty for three days and nights without even having time for a wash. And yet we were better off than the others. When night fell I got back to the Mosque, and was relieved next day.

# CHAPTER V

*Despondency and its cure : Defending the vegetable market : Wounded : My attempt to reach Rao's picket : A dangerous position : An invalid : A trying journey : Nerves : In a patent apparatus*

ON June 27 I was ordered for Hindoo Rao's picket. On that morning I got up in the very lowest spirits; never before or since have I been in such a bewildering state of depression. Besides being low-spirited I was also muddle-headed, and the Adjutant had to call attention to the mistakes I made on falling in my picket. It is enough to say that I felt supremely wretched and confident of disaster.

As we advanced, round shot and grape came crashing through the trees, and a big bough fell close to me ; then, in a moment, the whole black feeling of misery vanished, and I was myself again. Having arrived at Hindoo Rao's, I was ordered down to the Subsee Mundee (vegetable market), a collection of mud huts on both sides of the Grand Trunk road. These huts had thatched roofs, all of which had been burnt.

While wondering what to do in this vast assemblage of huts, I received an order from

## THE INDIAN MUTINY

the Commanding Officer of the picket telling me to hold the place with my men. In answer I wrote back at once that if he would send me a thousand men I should be happy to obey him, but with my force all I could hope to do was to try to defend the line of road. As there were three or four pukka buildings close to our side of the road I took possession of them, so that I might keep the road between me and the enemy's approach. Already I had heard that the enemy were streaming out of the Lahore Gate to attack me.

These buildings were detached, but they were only twenty or thirty yards apart, and I could readily talk from the one I was in to the next one. We barricaded the doors, and I posted most of the men on the roof, because some cover could be obtained from the three-foot parapets which were round the roofs of all these houses. On the first floor of my house there was only one door facing the road and, like all native doors, it was very small, and evidently had been connected with the ground by a ladder which had been destroyed.

As we had no entrenching tools whatever, I went to this doorway to examine the thickness of the wall and to see if the men could loophole it with their bayonets. While I was standing in the doorway about twenty sepoys fired a volley at me from the other side of the road. The bullets hit both the woodwork on which I was standing and that which my head was touching. They smashed against the brick wall by the side of my ear, and one bullet took me in the thigh diagonally and came out near my hip, and another hit a man by the name of James Hartley in the iliac artery.

At the moment I had my naked sword in my left hand, for the scabbard had been shot away. The volley made me start so violently that I drove my sword right through my left foot and through the sole of my boot, but of this I knew nothing whatever until some time afterwards.

I limped back from the doorway to find that my young subaltern and my colour-sergeant Noon were both crying. Language cannot express my feelings of rage at these men for shedding tears because I had been hit. I grabbed a pugaree, put a bullet into it, and made a rough tourniquet of it, twisting it very tight with a man's bayonet. Shortly afterwards I became conscious that James Hartley was bleeding to death. I saw the jetting of the artery, and getting down I put my thumb on it. Then, with the assistance of one of the men, I got

## THE INDIAN MUTINY

another pugaree and another bullet and tied him up as well as I could.

During this time I was both in frightful pain and as angry as a man can be. But in the way of misfortune things had reached a climax, for shortly afterwards we cleared the enemy off the opposite side of the road, and eventually they retired. When all was quiet again I posted my men carefully, and improved as far as was possible the facilities for firing to the front. Having also seen to the other buildings, I could not go on any longer, so I told Pay-Sergeant Brady that I should want him to come with me to Hindoo Rao's.

Leaning on Brady's shoulder, and using my sword as a walking-stick, I started and staggered along for perhaps a hundred yards. Then I felt that the only thing in the world for me to do was to sit down, and while I was resting on a conveniently low wall a spent grape-shot took me in the back between the shoulder-blades, and knocked all the breath out of me.

Struggle as I would I found that I could not get up the hill to the main picket, so when I had recovered breath enough to move I came in the rear of Hindoo Rao's. This was just the spot round which all the shells fell which had missed Hindoo Rao's, and having reached this inhospitable place, I discovered that I could not walk another yard. So, having sent Brady up the hill to get a hospital dooly, I lay down and waited.

There was, however, to be no good fortune for me on that day. Indeed Brady had scarcely gone before the enemy appeared on the other side of this plain, and seeing that I was the only object in the foreground, they immediately opened fire upon me. In the face of what seemed to me a terrific virulent hailstorm I crawled behind the biggest thistle I could find, and lay down with my head towards the enemy.

Now this bit of flat ground was commanded by the inlying picket, where, on a mound, an 8-inch howitzer and an 18-pounder had been placed. These weapons had been discarded from the front because, from constant firing, their vents had become enlarged. I did not, however, know this interesting fact, and so, while I lay behind my thistle attracting an attention which I was far from appreciating, I cursed the officer in command for not opening fire upon my assailants.

Afterwards I was told that the officer was waiting for a fancy shot, because as more and more of the enemy came up to have a pot at me he completely enfiladed them.

## THE INDIAN MUTINY

At last he let fly, and one round of grape from the howitzer and a shot from the 18-pounder did so much damage that not another shot was fired at me.

By this time Brady, with a dooly and four bearers, had come down from Hindoo Rao's, and when they had put down the dooly I managed to crawl into it. Hardly had I done so when a shell from Delhi pitched right into the ground underneath the dooly, whereupon the men, who were just getting me on their shoulders, dropped me on the top of the shell and fled. My first—and very natural—idea was to move, but I was in such pain that I could not. So I just waited, and I can most truthfully say that I did not care. I had gone through so much during the last few hours that to be sitting on the top of a shell seemed to be absolutely unalarming. As, however, nothing happened, the men soon returned and walked off with me. The hole in the ground was there for anyone to see, but luckily for us the fuse must have blown out. Without any more adventures or misadventures I at last reached the hospital.

There they probed the wound to get a part of my trousers out of the hole, and in the process gave me hospital gangrene, for there was no antiseptic treatment of any kind. They also discovered that my left boot was full of blood, and when they had cut it off I knew, for the first time, that the point of my sword had gone right through my foot. The doctor then told me that the hospital was already too full, and that it was best for me to be carried to my tent.

My wound was dressed only every other day, and I had to lie on a little charpoy, about four feet in length, on which I remained until the beginning of August. Then the senior surgeon came to me and said, " Look here, Harris, your leg will be no use to you in that crooked state. You had better let me divide everything underneath the knee, and give you a straight leg for life." To this I agreed at once, but when he began to spread out his knives and other paraphernalia, I changed my mind. " If you go cutting and carving me any more," I told him, " I shall go under. If I must have it done, won't it be better to send me up to the depôt, where I can have it cut off in a good climate, and without any flies to bother me ? "

" Quite right, Harris," he replied, and immediately began to shut up his knives.

The result of this was that a medical board was ordered, and on that same evening I started, with Jim Daniel, of the 1st

## THE INDIAN MUTINY

Fusiliers, in an "anna-a-miler" for Kurnaul. Daniel had been badly wounded in the right forearm, and we were put into this conveyance in such a way that I could not move, and it may well be imagined what a trying journey this was for us both.

We reached the dāk bungalow in the morning, and the change was so delightful that we both began to improve immediately, and I exercised myself by crawling about the floor. The monsoon was now in full swing, and altogether we spent three days in reaching Umballa, the last part of our journey being taken in a dooly. Owing to long disuse my legs, always very slight below the knee, had become a sight for curious beholders. Every bit of muscle I had ever had seemed to have faded away, and the cry of "Come and have a look at Jim Harris's legs" was a common one in camp.

We stayed with Dr. Jowett in Umballa for a few days, and very kind he was to us. From Umballa we travelled by dooly to Kalka, and from there by janpan to Subathoo.

When we were approaching the station the first man I saw was our young assistant surgeon, John Wilson, who had been left in charge of the depôt. "What have you come up for?" he asked me.

"Because the surgeon says you ought to divide everything under my knee, and give me a straight leg. He told me that this one will never be any use," I replied.

"Oh," he returned, "it will be time enough to do that when there is nothing else to be done."

My leg, however, was as firm as a rock, and I assured him that he would never get it to straighten out.

The quiet of this little hill station was astounding to me, and I quickly became aware that I had such things as nerves. While I had been lying for long weeks on that wretched little charpoy at Delhi, I had been well braced up and ready for anything. The sound of firing had been my constant companion, sometimes coming very near, sometimes far off. These sounds must have stimulated me, for if I could only have moved I should have been happy enough. But now I jumped at a sound, and could not understand the reason.

The morning after we arrived two natives came down from the hospital when I was lying on my charpoy, and said that the Doctor Sahib had sent them to rub my knee with oil.

"Rub my grandmother," I replied ungraciously, but I let them rub me for an

## THE INDIAN MUTINY

hour, and then the doctor, with two assistants, appeared. Thereupon I was strapped into what they called an "Amesbury's patent fracture apparatus," which fitted me from the sole of my foot to my hip-bone. It had a sort of wheel and axle acting underneath the knee-joint, which enlarged the angle, and they turned this until I could bear no more. In this machine I lived from sunrise to sunset for two months.

# CHAPTER VI

An expedition through the hill States : Frost-bite and snow-blindness : An avalanche : For once I get the better of Lord William Hay

MY leg became fairly straight after this, but it lost all retractile power. I was, however, able to go up to Simla in a janpan, and soon afterwards found that I could leave off one of my crutches.

Hodson's wife was up at Simla, and gave a most remarkable dinner party while I was there. Fourteen of us sat down to dinner, but only two of us were able to cut up our meat!

Delhi was taken by the middle of September, and I determined to join my regiment if it was going on any further service; but I found that the regiment was to be left in garrison. Order was quickly restored in Delhi and the neighbourhood.

Towards the end of the month Lord William Hay asked me to go with him on a tour through the hill States—an offer which I gladly accepted. We started during the first week in October, and, after marching for ten or twelve days, we came to a beautiful village. Thence we sent back our ponies and heavy baggage by Hay's bearer,

## THE INDIAN MUTINY

and told him to join us at the bungalow at Chini, which had been built in the Sutlej valley by Lord Dalhousie, the late Governor-General of India.

The next day we began the ascent of the Boorungathi pass, over 15,000 feet high. Having reached the limit of the birch, we camped at 12,000 feet in the snow. The pass had been closed on August 9, and every approach to it from the Indian side was through deep snow.

Warmed by hot coffee and toast, we started for the pass early next morning, and very hard work we found it. Indeed, "three steps and lie down" may be said to have been our programme. Forty men, without loads, were sent on ahead to make a path, and I had half a dozen men or more to pull me. They, however, were as useless at pulling as I was at climbing, and by the time I reached the top I was so exhausted that I said to myself, "If the pass is like this, and of any length, I shall never get through."

It was, therefore, an immense relief to find that the pass was wind-swept and only some forty yards across. By this time Hay, having some fine men with him who really were a help, was two hours ahead of me. But the way was now down-hill, and I made some very long slides and was able to rejoin Hay in the evening at a sæter.[1]

For hours I had not had any feeling in my feet, and on taking off my boots and stockings I found that my feet were badly frostbitten. So, while I was eating the largest *pâté de foie gras* I have ever seen, and drinking a bottle of champagne, Hay sent two natives to rub my legs with snow. I thought that I was bound to lose some portion of my feet, but in three weeks they were all right again. Three of our men lost their toes, the reason being that they would light fires and warm them.

We turned in to spend the night in a hay-loft, but as soon as the light was put out we were in agony from snow-blindness. On the next day Hay could not bear the light, and for forty-eight hours I had to keep him in darkness. My eyes being very strong, I did not suffer so much, and also I had tied a blue handkerchief round my head during most of the time we had been in the snow.

We were now up in very high land, and both of us felt magnificently fit. Each day we marched about thirty miles quite easily, and presently reached the borders of Tibet. The country was entirely Buddhist, and we

[1] A place where the people keep and milk their cows in summer.

# THE INDIAN MUTINY

passed several fine monasteries. At one of these the monks held a service for us, a sort of high mass, with a lot of weird brass instruments of music. Possibly I was mistaken, but I must say that these monks did not seem to be in the least devout. Altogether we covered a good deal of country and crossed two high passes, which are, I have been told, higher than Mont Blanc; but as they were not so deeply covered with snow, we made light of them.

Returning by the Sutlej valley, we reached the bungalow, which was situated in a beautiful spot sloping down through easy-terraced cultivation to the river; and there we were met by our ponies and baggage. On the other side of the river lay the village of Poaree, which nestled at the foot of the tremendous Khylas peaks. These peaks are 24,000 feet high, and their sides, to a height of about 12,000 feet, are clothed with grand forests of deodars.

This bungalow was only 120 to 130 miles from Simla, and as Hay had a chuprassie who could do his ninety miles a day in a go-as-you-please style, we soon got our letters. Then I found that my regiment was still garrisoned at Delhi, and that there was no necessity for me to rejoin until the expiration of my leave.

We had only been at the bungalow for a short time when, whilst writing on the verandah, we suddenly heard a most terrific noise. It seemed to me like whole batteries of guns being thrown down the rocks. Hay shouted to me, "Look over there, Jim, at that avalanche." I looked across at the mountains, but my eyes were trying to find one spot, and several seconds passed before I realised that this avalanche was tearing through the enormous forest of deodars over a width of nearly two miles. I have never seen a more wonderful or more impressive sight.

Leaving the bungalow, we soon parted from the Sutlej, and had to go a long way round to get back to it. The river itself flowed through a quite impassable country, but we came to it again at the Wangtoo Bridge. This bridge belonged to the Rajah of Busahir, who lived at Rampur, about fifty miles below. It crossed the river just beneath the spot where the Sutlej comes through the main chain of the Himalayas. The Sutlej comes through a terrific gorge at about an angle of $45°$, and carries boulders of ten and twenty tons like marbles.

At a place where the rocks on either side made the stream narrower, the Rajah had placed three tiers of large tree trunks on

## THE INDIAN MUTINY

both banks, one tier above another, and each one projecting from the one below it. On the top of these, stretching from one bank to the other, he had placed the largest deodar in the country.

The approaches on each side were covered with earth, and the tree itself had footholds, which had been cut with native adzes for bare-footed people to cross over.

There had always been a pleasant rivalry between Hay and myself about riding across impossible (or, at any rate, unlikely) places. He being my senior, and I being only a " griff," he was inclined to show me what horrible places could be ridden over if only one had the audacity to try. At this time he had a most beautiful pair of grey ponies, Shalka and Shamma, and he was riding one and I the other.

I was a fair distance ahead of Hay when I came to the bridge, and I started to cross it. When I reached the middle of it I did not think it possible to go any farther, for the tree began to taper considerably towards the other side. I remember taking my feet almost out of the stirrups, and, while keeping the reins from hanging, I put both hands on my pony's withers, meaning, if he slipped, to throw myself back and try to land astride on the tree. As far as I could see there

## REMINISCENCES

seemed to be nothing in front of the pony for him to walk upon. But we got across.

When Hay came to the bridge he consulted with his hill people and the Rajah's head man. The latter said, " No man has ever ridden across this bridge. Nobody has ever tried to. They say that your friend has ridden across it, but do not attempt to follow him."

Hay dismounted, and with men holding ropes in front and behind him, he walked across in his stockinged feet. Then he came up and asked me if I had ridden across, and after I had answered he turned away and said no more. But that was the only time I ever got the better of him.

Only a few years ago, when I was at the Delhi dinner on June 8, Colonel L. Wavell came to me and said, "Are you the man who rode over the Wangtoo?" And when I said "Yes," he replied, " I wonder how you could ! I came to that bridge on my way back from Kooloo ; my leave was nearly up and I had no time to spare. Yet I stayed two days before I could make up my mind to cross. Finally I went over on my hands and knees ! "

## CHAPTER VII

Young "bloods" : A risky ride : Ill-feeling : I win some money and lose it again

PROCEEDING on our tour, Hay and I got down to Rampur, where there was a long reach of level water and I found another method of crossing the Sutlej. The natives crossed on mussuks, and a mussuk was the skin of a cow blown out with air and the neck of it made airtight. The ferryman lay across this, and if you wanted to go to the other side of the river you sat on the small of his back and kept your feet on the skin. To me this method had the advantage of being delightfully simple and easy.

I have not remarked upon the sport which we enjoyed during this trip, but the Rajahs of every State always made a point of giving us a big drive. On the whole our bag was a very fair one, and consisted of a few bears and some small game which included many different kinds of the Himalayan pheasant.

We got back to Simla in the first week of January 1858, and I went to stay with Dr. Peskett, who was the Civil Surgeon, and his charming wife. Now Peskett was a great man for good ponies, and had, in fact, more of them than he could exercise. So one afternoon he said to me, "I wish you would exercise a pony I have got. He is a very good one and came originally from Spiti"—which place was about as far up towards Tibet as Hay and I had been.

The pony was a dun, about 14.1, with a black mane and tail, and very powerful. I rode him along the Mall at a sharp canter, and thought that Peskett's opinion of him was quite correct. The afternoon was damp and drizzly, and as I rode up to the reading-room I found a group of all the young bloods in Simla — Bashi Bazouk Evans, Johnny Chadwick of the 9th Lancers, Fawcett of the Bays, King Harman, Edwardes of the Rifles, and some others.

On the other side of the Mall, opposite to the rooms, was a high wall; and set, as it were, in the wall was a flight of steps, bound with wood and about sixty feet high. So narrow were the steps that I could only just get half my foot on any one of them, and each step was some thirteen inches in height. These steps led up to the Pavilion Hotel, and they used to come down every year during the rains.

When I joined the group I have mentioned, I heard someone say, "You won't believe it, but I saw a native horse-dealer

## THE INDIAN MUTINY

ride up those steps on a little twelve-hand pony this morning." I do not know what made me say what I did, but I promptly replied, " I do not think much of that. I'll ride up—and down them, too—if you will make it worth my while." These young bloods clearly thought that they had found an easy way to make money, for in a moment one of them said, " I bet you 500 rupees you don't," and then another added, " And I'll bet you 400." Then three others joined in with offers to bet me 400, 200, and 100 rupees.

" Have you all done ? I'll take the lot of you. Stand back and give me room," was my reply, when no more bets seemed to be forthcoming.

Now, owing to the narrowness of the Mall opposite to the steps, I could not get a straight run at them, so I took a slant and rushed the pony towards them. I got up to the top directly, for my mount was extremely strong, but to come down was altogether a different matter.

On the top there was a small plateau, not much bigger than a large dining-table, and on this I turned the pony round and looked down. The view, however, only made me think that I had made a fool of myself, for it seemed to me that we simply must topple over while attempting to make such a steep descent. However, I made up my mind that if the pony put his foot down the first step he should go. He started all right and, sitting quite still, I went down with the greatest ease, for he sat down behind, and descended by using his forelegs only, his hind feet being on each side of my face.

When we were about half-way down, one of the men below called out, " Well, I value my life at more than a thousand rupees"—a sneer which leads me to add that, after the Mutiny, there was a good deal of ill-feeling between the Queen's officers and those of the Company's army. The former pretended to look down upon us, because we were Company's officers, and also because the Army had mutinied.

I never have been able to put up with that sort of thing, so I felt that I had not spent quite an agreeable afternoon. On the next morning I was paid the whole of my money, and I lost it again at loo the next night.

This feeling between the forces lasted for some years, and did not die out until the Queen took over the whole army. We of the Company's European Regiment were the more annoyed at the contempt showered

## THE INDIAN MUTINY

upon us because we had not mutinied, and we were immensely proud of our regiment, which we considered to be better dressed, better drilled, and more fit for hard work than the Line.

## CHAPTER VIII

Digging for treasure in Delhi : Prize auctions : I gain some valuable knowledge : The old King and his habits : On leave : Richard Shebbeare : I join the 15th Punjabees : Our journey to Lucknow : Examinations : The Nana and a letter to W. H. Fitchett

LEAVING Simla, I rejoined my regiment at Delhi in the first week of February, and found that all my brother officers were quartered in the palace. I myself was given a couple of rooms in the Zenana of the King. The quarter-guard was near the Dewan Khas, next to which we all lived, the 60th Rifles and ourselves dividing the duties between us.

It was here that, shortly after my arrival, it was written up in chalk, "Delhi taken and India saved for 36 rupees, 12 annas." My memory may play me false about the exact amount, but the one I have given is approximately correct. It meant that, by the orders of the Government, the troops engaged were allowed six months' batta. This simple sentence was sent to England and appeared in the newspapers, with the result that the Government immediately gave us another six months' batta.

The city and the neighbourhood were quite quiet by this time, although, if one

## THE INDIAN MUTINY

went out early in the morning, twenty or thirty natives could be seen hanging in the Chandni Chonk.

Life was rather dull, but we could get leave from the prize agents to dig for treasure, on a percentage, in the houses of rebels. I unluckily never found anything, but I remember digging in the house of a man called Achmit Pie. I dug on a Monday on one side of the lintel of an inner room and found nothing. On the following Wednesday somebody else, acting on better information, dug on the other side of the doorway and found 60,000 rupees and three bottles of quicksilver.

Our greatest excitement was to attend the prize auctions, which were held twice a week in a large hall. The procedure was as follows: The auctioneer and his men, accompanied by one of the agents, brought in several large boxes, which contained all sorts of jewellery and treasures. Most of the Europeans and some of the loyal natives sat at a very long table, while others stood around. The auctioneer produced three old soup plates, worth about 2$d$. each. These he filled from the boxes, and each plate was passed round for us to inspect; then it was put up to auction and knocked down to the highest bidder.

I attended a great number of these auctions, and at various times bought many soup plates at very various prices, my maximum, I think, being 1200 rupees for a plateful. I often wish I had kept my purchases, for they would be worth a great deal more now than I ever got for them. The native jewellers used to come round to our quarters nearly every day, squat on the floor beside their jewellery, which was all more or less adapted for the European market, and either try to buy our purchases or get us to exchange them for their own wares. These natives doubtless got very much the best of it, but I gained a knowledge of values which was subsequently to be of considerable service to me.

One of our duties—and it amused me—was very often to be on guard over the old King, Bahadur Shah, the last of the Great Moguls. He had two of his wives with him and his youngest son, Jumma Bukht. Our orders were to see him personally at least three times a day. He and I had many talks together, and he was, I think, quite a harmless old man, whose chief delight was to make Persian poetry.

His son, however, seemed to be just a common kind of scoundrel, whose three elder brothers, as all the world knows, had

## THE INDIAN MUTINY

been captured early in the siege, and shot by Hodson, near Humayon's tomb. Hodson has been cruelly blamed for this action, but I feel sure that every man in the camp, of my acquaintance at least, would have been glad of such a chance. I most certainly should.

The old King used to be very violently and daily sick into a gold basin. But when I offered him my sympathy, he assured me that there was no cause, as, for the last two-and-thirty years, he could not eat his dinner until he had gone through this performance.

In the late spring the Colonel gave me three months' leave, and asked me to go up to Subathoo to take to pieces and pack up the billiard table, and send it down to Delhi. From want of skilled labour I experienced some difficulty over this job, but at last I despatched the table to Delhi, and then went up to Simla.

There I made the acquaintance of Robert Shebbeare, who had received orders from the Punjab Government to raise a regiment of Musbee Sikhs—a low-caste kind of Sikh, that had not previously been enlisted by the Government. I saw a great deal of Shebbeare, and admired him very much. He had belonged to the 60th Native Infantry, which was one of the regiments that had mutinied at Umballa.

Shebbeare asked me if I would like to join his regiment, the 15th Punjabees, and I was only too delighted to accept his offer. The regiment was then on the march down to Lucknow, under the second in command, Lieutenant W. Randall. Shebbeare, the Pesketts, and I rode across the hills to Mussoorie, and half way there we had to cross the Tons river on a single rope; hung on this rope was a little bit of V-shaped hard wood, from the two ends of which a loop depended, and in this we sat and were pulled across by a string. I was greatly pleased because Mrs. Peskett asked me to carry her baby over.

From Mussoorie we went down by dāk-gharrie as quickly as possible to Lucknow, and we joined the regiment at Ali Nuckee Khan's house in the first week of September 1858. This house was an enormous place, and held the whole of the regiment (about 840 men) quite easily. Sir Hope Grant was in command at Lucknow, and Wolseley was his Quartermaster-General. I saw a great deal of these officers, especially of Wolseley.

An unwelcome surprise awaited me in Lucknow, for a General Order was issued

## THE INDIAN MUTINY

to the effect that all officers, except those belonging to European regiments, must pass the P.H. examination or go back to their regiments. Up to this time I had never bothered about examinations, and indeed had never passed one in my life, for on entering the service all that had been required of me was a medical certificate, and that was given me by our old family doctor.

Now, however, I had to set to work, and just what might have happened if the examination had not been easy and my commanding officer one of the examining committee is not worth guessing. At any rate my commanding officer announced openly that he was not going to allow his Adjutant to be spun. But in spite of this assurance I was greatly relieved when I found that I had passed, and could therefore be confirmed as Adjutant of the 15th.

In the cold weather of '58–'59, I was sent off with three companies of Sikhs, and joined the army which was pursuing the Nana, at Byram Ghat. In connection with the Nana I beg leave to insert a letter which I wrote to the Rev. W. H. Fitchett in 1907 :

" History never yet has been written, and never will be, without mistakes, and I am not concerned to rectify trifles. One thing only I would mention, as I am sure it would be interesting to you, and it is known only to my family and to a few friends, mostly, if not all, dead. You say: 'No one knows where or how the Nana died.' I will tell you; but to do so I must give you a short sketch of myself.

"I was a subaltern in the 2nd E.B. Fusiliers, and returned to India from sick leave in England, in the cold weather of '56–'57; I stayed for some weeks at Cawnpore on my way up to join my regiment at Umballa. I knew the Nana quite well, having been introduced to him at Cawnpore as far back as '51.

"When the Mutiny broke out I was with my regiment at Subathoo, and marched down to Delhi with them. The first fight was at Bad-li-ke-serai, on June 8, and I was on the Ridge, &c., &c., and was badly wounded, and left for Subathoo again, apparently a hopeless cripple. But I got right again, and in 1858 was appointed Adjutant of the 15th Musbee Sikhs, and marched with them to Lucknow, arriving early in October.

"In November I was ordered, with a detachment of three companies, first to Byram Ghat and then to a ford on the Upper Gogra, called Chilari Ghat. A small party of seventeen Royal Engineers, under

# THE INDIAN MUTINY

Richard Harrison (now General Sir Richard), presently joined me, with orders to construct a bridge, and a regiment of Pioneers, unarmed, with a lieutenant in command, were sent to help. I commanded the whole.

"Now these Musbees had never been enlisted by Government before; they were lowcaste men, all—or almost all—expert thieves and trackers. I had a guard of them always at the ford, and lived myself in a tent close by. This ford was only about thirty miles from the Terai, into which the rebel forces with the Nana had been driven, and for the deserters from his force it was the most convenient way by which to get back to Western Oude, or Rohilcund. Moreover, it was the only one where they would not meet some European force.

"Very shortly I found that, through my native officers, I was thoroughly posted up in all the Nana's movements. There was, as you know, a lac of rupees reward for his head, dead or alive. Two of my subahdars were always at me to allow them three or four days' leave to capture him. They kept me informed of his movements, like a *Court Circular*. I always told them that I was on duty for a certain purpose, and that it was impossible for me to give any man leave.

"One Thursday Ram Sing came to me,

begging me still more strongly than before, and saying that the Nana was getting much worse—he was, as I knew, suffering from fever and ague, and had an enlarged spleen. Ram Sing also told me that the Nana had had his little finger cut off, and had burnt it as an offering to Kali, with the view of propitiating the goddess.

"Two days after, Ram Sing and the other subahdar came to me and said: 'No one will get the reward now; he died and was burnt yesterday.' And I feel quite sure that was true, for I had known for some weeks about all his movements."

I have regretted ever since that I was, on this occasion, such a stickler for obedience to orders, which were to guard the ford and to protect the bridge about to be built. Had I listened to the advice of native officers, and taken some thirty men and a couple of sowars, with an ekka, I am confident that I should have captured the Nana. And I expect that, if I had been successful, the blame would not have been very much; while, if I had been lucky enough to get a brevet, the whole of my career would have been altered.

The bridge was built principally of very large bamboos, and just when it was finished the river changed its course. This occurred

# THE INDIAN MUTINY

two or three times, so the necessity for the bridge having apparently passed away, we were recalled to Byram Ghat. There we found a considerable force, and I was directed to assume charge of the treasure-chest, which meant that I was to find the money from the Civil Government for the pay of the troops. Now, by the Bengal regulations, I was entitled to 300 rupees a month for doing this, but I never got a pice.

After a month or so the force broke up, and I was ordered to march my detachment to Faizabad and report myself. When about half-way there a terrific storm of rain came on, and the ditches on each side of the road were filled to overflowing. We found these ditches to be full immediately of small fish, like whitebait, which were excellent to eat. As we were miles away from any river, and as the country previously had been quite dry, where these fish came from was, and is, a mystery to me.

# CHAPTER IX

*Faizabad : The Fakir and his powers : Back to Lucknow : Ordered to China : Irritating delays : A quick steamer : Lively times at Singapore : Arrival in China : A sharp but brief dispute : Wolseley : In clover : Feats of strength : Oysters*

FAIZABAD was a nice place, quite well wooded, and much cooler than Lucknow. The D.A.Q.M.G. gave me leave to camp where I liked near the Grand Parade, so I took possession of a fine Tope of mango trees.

There were more snakes and scorpions in Faizabad than in any other place I ever saw. Even riding across the parade ground, a perfectly bare plain without a bit of cover, one would see several snakes curled up, presumably asleep. And I can vouch for the fact that a little bit of carpet, by the side of my charpoy, generally had a scorpion or two underneath it.

We had just pitched camp and made ourselves comfortable when one of the native officers, who had come up to report "All right," said to me, " Sahib, have you seen the Fakir, sitting between five fires? He sits on the bare plain, between four cow-dung fires, the sun being the fifth. If you will step up on to this mound [which was

# THE INDIAN MUTINY

within a few yards of my tent at the corner of the Tope], I will show him to you."

We stood on the mound, and about 500 yards away I saw an object, which was evidently the Fakir. The native officers knew something of the man, and they told me that he was a Sikh of high caste, who had made a vow to sit between five fires from sunrise to sunset, during all the hot season, for nine years. They also suggested that if I wished to see him after sunset, I should find the Fakir seated in a chair on the open plain dressed in clean white garments, with a disciple near him. His hair was reported to be 18 cubits and his beard 12 cubits in length.

I was greatly interested, and on that evening, with a couple of native officers and my orderly carrying a chair, I went up and had a talk with the Fakir. He had slight fever, and I asked after his health, and why he went through such tortures. His reply was that he wished to lead the higher life and to obtain powers. Then he took down his beard, which had been done up into a plait on his chin, and placed it in my hand, a mark of very great confidence. It would have been rude to have measured his beard, but I have no doubt that it was, as I had been told, fully 18 feet long.

We continued to talk, and he told me that he would be free as soon as the rains fell, and that they generally began between June 27 and 30. He wore sandals, with no sides whatever to them, and while we were talking I noticed a large scorpion close to his foot. "Don't move," I said quietly, "there is a scorpion close to your foot." He leant over, saw the scorpion, pointed with his fingers in its direction, and immediately it shrivelled up and died.

"You seem to have some powers already," I remarked, but he simply waved the matter aside as being of no importance.

My interview with the Fakir took place in May, and we had a very wet march back to Lucknow, where we arrived in the middle of July '59, and rejoined the regiment.

Parades, mess dinners, races, and the usual routine of cantonment life made the time pass until the cold weather began. Then Sir Hope Grant informed us that a force of 10,000 men from India was to go to China in the early spring, and that our regiment was to go, because the Government particularly wished to test these Musbee Sikhs.

This was delightful news, but a long time went by before we started. We heard of other regiments marching down to Calcutta and going off, and wondered whether we

## THE INDIAN MUTINY

should be left behind. At last, however, we marched down the Grand Trunk road, and arrived at Calcutta in January. There again we were delayed, and had the mortification of seeing all the other troops sent off to China before us.

At length the regiment was ordered to embark on a P. & O. paddle-steamer, but she could not hold all of us, so once more I had the vexation of being left behind in charge of about 130 men. Eight young officers had been attached to us for service in China, one to each company, and Shebbeare, always good-natured, gave me my choice, as I, at least, was entitled to one of them. I chose Fred Sotheby, of the Rifle Brigade, and he was my chum through the whole campaign.

Eventually we embarked, though we were the last of the force to start, but we had the luck to go in the screw-steamer *Lightning*. She was an opium clipper, engaged in the trade of smuggling opium into China, and one of the fastest vessels afloat. So by the time we got to Singapore we had left half the force behind us.

We were detained at Singapore for several days, and had a most lively time. One hundred and fifty transports were in the Straits, besides many vessels of the Royal

Navy. Every night we used to dine on shore, and some of those dinners were as merry as they were unceremonious. The fact was that we youngsters were rather offended at the tone of the senior officers of the Navy towards their younger officers, and when we suspected that they were trying to snub us we determined not to submit to their rudeness.

I remember that at a big dinner at the Oriental, one of the largest hotels, we cheered the French admiral most vociferously, and then chaired him all round the table. Later on, we tossed the landlord in his own blanket and in front of his own entrance door.

Transports were leaving every day for Hong Kong, but we were no longer annoyed at being left behind because we knew that we could catch them up; and the *Lightning* turned out to be the first vessel to arrive in China. From the date of our arrival all the troops were put on Indian pay, a circumstance which pleased everyone and took place on April 17.

We landed at Kowloon, on the mainland, just opposite to Hong Kong. It was then nothing but grass; now I believe it is entirely covered with houses. There we soon made ourselves at home, for we had our tents with us. Troops of all sorts were continually

# THE INDIAN MUTINY

coming in, and very soon quite a large force was collected there.

After five weeks or so transport after transport began to sail for the north, our destination being Ta-lien-whan, in Manchuria. Again, however, I was left behind. The regiment went off, as before, in the *Bentinck*, but now I had four companies with me, and Shebbeare having been invalided home, I was left in command. Nevertheless I was far from satisfied at being left behind.

Then, when I was brooding over my disappointment, I suddenly got an order from Wolseley, Quartermaster-General of the Force, to take my Sikhs and command the troops on board the *Impératrice*. Now the *Impératrice* was the finest transport of all, and had been employed to lay the Red Sea cable. A small steamer took us alongside, and I, going on board first, was received at the gangway by an officer, who gave his name as Major B——.

"Are you Lieutenant Harris?" he asked, and when I had admitted that I was, he asked me if I had come to command the troops on board. Again I replied with the solid word "Yes," and then he continued: "I must tell you, sir, that we object to being commanded by a subaltern. We have two or three majors, two colonels, and several captains on board belonging to the Commissariat or Land Transport Column. We have no objection to your having the best cabin, but we object to being commanded by a subaltern." "Well," I replied, "I have my orders and am going to command. I think the best plan will be to go down below at once, and see to the accommodation for all these troops. I understand that there will be two thousand men on board, and detachments of the Artillery and of all the regiments that have gone on. When I have made my arrangements I will come up to the saloon, and will then issue my orders. You will, of course, do just as you think right, but you will have to give me your decision in writing."

When I returned from my duties several of the seniors said that they did not object to my orders as orders, but that they would not be commanded by a junior officer. And when they had written down something to this effect, I gave it to my orderly and sent it off at once to Wolseley.

We played whist and spent quite a pleasant evening together. They were, indeed, a capital lot of fellows, and before the evening was over I was able to chaff them about the wigging I thought that they would get on the morrow. And my expectations were

# THE INDIAN MUTINY

realised, for about 7 A.M. on the next morning Wolseley and the Adjutant-General and a lot of the staff came on board.

Wolseley immediately took me aside and said, "I say, Jim, don't make it too hard for these fellows. You know they are senior, but they are all non-combatant, and you have to command."

"My dear fellow," I answered, "I am sure it will be all right, but I could not go on, you see, until the point was settled. It is quite evident that someone must command, and as I have got the order I am going to do so."

"Well," Wolseley assured me, "they are going to get the d——est wigging they have ever had in their lives."

After this, I never had any more trouble, and everything went as smoothly as possible. I had a cabin fit for a king, and a boat of four oars at my disposal day and night. Altogether I was in clover. I do not suppose that we went very fast, as we had four transports and a gunboat in tow, but there was no particular hurry, and in the course of time we arrived at Ta-lien-whan, a magnificent harbour, almost landlocked, and some seventy miles around.

We landed about 8000 men, where the town of Dalny now stands. At that time there was only a small Tartar village, the inhabitants of which kept us well supplied with mutton and vegetables. They also took great interest in the Sikhs, and never missed a single parade. In our regiment we had a good many wrestlers, and the Tartars were delighted to see them going through their exercises.

We had, also, an enormous mugdur,[1] which only our strongest men could raise above their heads. The villagers were most anxious to try this feat, and greatly to the astonishment of the Sikhs every Tartar lifted the mugdur quite easily. Then they brought a big stone and put it on the parade ground, but not one of our men could lift it, though half a dozen of the Tartars managed to do so.

On landing at this place I saw, with great pleasure, that the whole coast was covered with oysters—real natives. I at once sent back a message to the Chief Engineer by the coxswain of the boat I had landed from, asking him to send me a bucket and an oyster-knife. Later on I got a hammer and a chisel, and next morning the beach was a sight with 8000 men eating oysters. Not only the troops, but many of the Royal Navy and the crews of the transports joined

[1] Indian club used for exercise.

# THE INDIAN MUTINY

in the fun. Two days afterwards one had to walk for miles before finding an oyster.

We stayed at Ta-lien-whan for about five weeks. The climate was glorious, the scenery beautiful, and the food excellent. We had no sickness, and during the whole campaign I do not believe we ever had more than three men at a time in the hospital. Truly, the China campaign of 1860 was the most enjoyable picnic in which I have ever taken part.

## CHAPTER X

Peh-tang : A comfortable rut : The Government pawn-
broking establishment : Mud : We take the Taku Forts

WE did not see much of our cavalry at Ta-lien-whan, for they were on the other side of the great bay. We bought, however, a capital gig from the captain of the *Bentinck*, and in this we used frequently to sail and row, and made excursions not only to Odin Bay (where the cavalry were), but also to the very inner end of Ta-lien-whan, to a village which became famous in the great campaign between the Japanese and Russians. For there the former won a great battle, preparatory to their investment of Port Arthur.

All this time we were waiting for the French, who were at Chefoo, on the mainland of Shan-tung, but, as far as my memory serves me, I think that we re-embarked in August. No longer was I relegated to the splendid *Impératrice*. Indeed, my lot was very different, for I had to embark on the humble *Forerunner*, a 600-ton barque, hailing from Sunderland. Her charter-party was but £50 a day, instead of the £500 of the *Impératrice*. She just held our left wing, and we had her all to ourselves. I had a

## THE INDIAN MUTINY

stern cabin, but I could not stand upright in it.

We sailed out of the great harbour, and formed up in five long lines, each line being headed by one of Her Majesty's ships. Smaller craft were on the right flank. We steamed close past Port Arthur, and, having been joined by the French, we entered the Gulf of Pe-chi-li. Then, having arrived opposite the Taku Forts, we anchored a little to the north of them, in the same long lines, parallel to the shore, at about two miles distant.

When everything was in order, we sailed north for a few miles up the coast, until we were opposite to a place called Peh-tang, where the water was very shallow. Then, in gunboats, and boats towed by them, we landed on a sand-bank, just under the walls of Peh-tang. Apparently there were a great number of guns on these walls, but all of them turned out to be dummies, and no opposition was made to our landing. The sand on which we landed had more than an inch of water upon it, and, as far as we could judge, the only dry place was a raised road, which evidently went from the gate of Peh-tang to the Taku Forts. We immediately steered for this road.

The General Commanding would not

allow us to enter Peh-tang, presumably because it was rather late in the afternoon. Consequently, the whole of the infantry of the First Division lay down to spend the night on the road. The road was covered with charmingly soft mud, and, lying lengthways in a rut with a thin waterproof sheet underneath me, I was as comfortable as anyone could wish to be. Unfortunately, some Tartar cavalry appeared close to us in the middle of the night, and we had all to stand to our arms. When we lay down again two hours afterwards, I had lost the rut which had fitted me so beautifully, and found that I was lying on the slanting bank of the road, and that my feet were continually slipping into the water of the ditch.

At daylight, the General having discovered that no opposition was to be expected, we all marched into Peh-tang, and found that it was a frightfully dirty place. All the roads were two feet deep in the blackest of mud.

We, however, were particularly lucky, for the Government pawnbroking establishment was in the street allotted to us, and this building, entirely enclosed within high walls, was quite the best in the town. In it were five or six great warehouses, which contained at least half the furniture, clothing, and

# THE INDIAN MUTINY

necessaries of all the inhabitants of Peh-tang and its neighbourhood.

We lived in the gateway, which was the sole entrance to this gigantic emporium. The gateway was paved with blue bricks, and the whole place was covered in with substantial awnings. Rooms on each side had raised platforms at one end, and these were permeated with flues, which, however, were not in use at this season of the year.

It was soon discovered that there was a sort of canal or creek by which the gunboats could come right up into Peh-tang, and I think that even some of the transports managed to get up. The French also landed, and their guns being heavier than ours, they had exceedingly hard work in dragging them, gun by gun, through the filthy streets.

To watch our artillery land was really a glorious sight. There was just room on a bit of dry bank to get the horses harnessed to the guns, and as soon as the men had mounted they started off at a gallop, and got to their encampment on the other side of the town in less than five minutes. Surely never were men, horses, guns, and limbers so covered with black mud.

When the Second Division and all the ammunition and stores had landed, the First

Division with the cavalry marched through country, which consisted of salt, mud, and graves, for the Taku Forts. We got to the rear of these forts without any opposition, and encamped for the night. The forts were on both sides of the Pei-ho River, and all their guns were directed seawards. We heard afterwards that the Chinese General had reported to the Emperor that the barbarians, being very ignorant of warfare, had been foolish enough to attack from that side. Next day the Second Division had their turn, and were ordered to attack the forts.

There were, I think, five forts, and during the night the enemy managed to turn some of their guns in our direction. But our real difficulty did not come from guns, but from mud, for the forts were surrounded by mud of an extraordinary depth. We had, however, some planks and scaling-ladders, and the latter were carried by the Chinese coolies, who, though unarmed, quite enjoyed the fun. Several of them were killed, but this only seemed to increase the delight of those who were not hurt. All the forts were taken by the evening, and we encamped in gardens on the left bank of the Pei-ho.

These gardens stretched for three or four

# THE INDIAN MUTINY

miles, and were full of the most delicious peaches. China is, I believe, the home of the peach, and these gardens were the property of the Emperor, and contained the finest peaches in the whole country. To see, first of all, 8000 men devouring oysters, and then to see them eating peaches, are sights which, to put it mildly, one does not expect during a campaign.

## CHAPTER XI

On the way to Pekin : The French General in danger : The punishment that failed : My first experience of looting : Tientsin : Capture of guns : Treating for peace : Treachery : Attacking the enemy : A clump of Tartars : A slap in the face : My report and its fate

BEFORE we left Peh-tang we had been formed into two divisions, each of two brigades. We became the Second Brigade, First Division, Sir John Michell commanding the division and Colonel Sutton our brigade. I cannot call to mind the arrangements of the artillery, the sappers, and the land transsport, though I knew most of the officers very well indeed.

Our brigade consisted of the 2nd Queen's and the 2nd, 15th, and 60th Sikhs, and here I would like to say that I am writing without a single book of reference, and so I beg to be pardoned if my memory fails me as to the sequence of events on the march up to Pekin.

The first event of any importance was an attack on the line of march by a large force of Tartar cavalry. We deployed as quickly as we could, and when our movement was completed my wing was on the left of the whole line. The French General, Mont-

# THE INDIAN MUTINY

auban, was nearly cut off by this body of cavalry, but fortunately he had behind him an escort of a troop under Lieutenant McGregor, who charged the Tartars at the critical moment, and saved both Montauban and the situation.

For this assistance the General was very grateful, and most strongly recommended McGregor for a brevet, and he got it. This was extraordinary because he was the only man in the whole force who got anything in the way of honours or rewards; the reason for this abstinence or parsimony, call it what you will, being that the *Times* correspondent (Bowlby) and our Commander-in-Chief quarrelled, and no one was recommended during the whole campaign.

The D.S.O. was then unknown, or, perhaps, some of us might have got that. But when I think of the abundance of honours and brevets that have been given in more recent campaigns, I cannot help feeling that we had rather hard luck.

One very curious incident on this march is stamped indelibly upon my memory. At a halting place the Provost-Marshal caught one of our 3000 Chinese coolies in the act of looting, a thing which had been strenuously forbidden. The culprit was tried by court-martial, and condemned to be hanged by way of example. The Chinese were drawn up on three sides of a hollow square, the scaffold was erected, and, preceded by his coffin according to the usual formula, the man was duly hanged.

But the result of this was not at all what we expected, for the whole of the Chinese coolies burst into the most uproarious laughter, and obviously considered that the whole proceeding was delightfully comical. As a spectacle they thought it first-rate, but as a deterrent it was the most dismal of all failures. Needless to say we had no more parades of the sort after this one.

Some days after we came to a large town, called Hose-woo, and here I received my first lesson in looting, for I found myself in orders to take a hundred rank and file and loot the Government pawnbroking establishment, so that we might obtain sufficient warm clothing for the native troops.

I thought that this would be an easy task, but my surmise was wrong. The building was approached by a long passage, and having walked down this to reconnoitre, I put my head into the yard at the end. Then I returned at once, and with fixed bayonets formed line as best I could, and drove everyone else out of the place at the point of the bayonet. A scene of the wildest disorder

## THE INDIAN MUTINY

followed. Men of every regiment in the service were looting and fighting. Two Chinese were killed, and many of the Europeans were wounded. A weapon which everyone seemed to be using with great effect was made from strings of copper cash. These weapons flew about in all directions, but were, perhaps, aimed especially at my head.

Very soon, however, I managed to get this nondescript crowd out of the place, and to post a strong guard at the gate. Then we helped ourselves to warm clothing, most of which consisted of sheepskin jackets. In Hose-woo we burnt some large warehouses full of brick tea, but I do not think that this wanton act was done intentionally.

About this time the enemy asked for a truce, and we granted their request; but we told the mandarins who came to treat that we intended to continue our march to Tientsin. When we arrived at this very large town on the Pei-ho we camped on a plain, near the river, and the country people most readily brought in supplies. We could buy a banghy load of fine grapes, certainly weighing two hundred pounds, for an empty bottle, and solid blocks of ice were to be obtained for the same price!

The gunboats came up the river as far as

this, and we could communicate easily with the fleet, which was anchored off the Taku Forts. My chief remembrance of Tientsin is the extraordinary number of frightful beggars abounding there. The truce, however, did not last very long, and we resumed our march west towards Pekin.

At some place on the road, called, I think, Chankiawan, where there was a fine bridge, we found the enemy in very strong force. There must have been at least 30,000 men, and we deployed to face them. Here again I found myself on the left of the line, for the General almost invariably split up my regiment into its two wings, so that I was given independent command.

Inclining my men a little to the left, we were soon completely separated from the rest of the army. Across our front was a very high and long bund, exactly like a large railway embankment, and I expect that it had something to do with the floods of the Hoang Ho river. Through this, about a mile or more ahead, there was a gap, and while making for this, I saw, alongside and under the bund, three guns, each drawn by two horses tandem fashion, with some twenty-five foot-men, armed only with swords, to each gun.

I was the only mounted man of our force,

## THE INDIAN MUTINY

so, having given Sotheby an order to bring up a couple of companies as quickly as possible, I galloped off to the gap. The Chinese, however, succeeded in getting the first gun through the gap, but I arrived in time to stop the others, and riding in front of the leading gun with revolver in hand, I kept on shouting "Kowtow," which was the only Chinese word in my vocabulary. I do not suppose that they understood my attempt at their language, but at any rate it had the effect of making them halt. Indeed, had they moved, I intended to shoot the leading pony through the head, but they seemed quite unable to make up their minds what to do, and made no attempt to advance or retire.

At the end of an awkward quarter of an hour my men began to straggle up at the double, and I told them to disarm all the Chinese. Had I given the order they would have killed the whole lot, but having disarmed them, I allowed them to go, and then we marched back with the guns.

One of these guns was a most curious specimen. It consisted of three barrels each six feet long, and carrying a two-ounce ball, but as they could be neither elevated nor depressed the gun did not seem to be of any very great use outside a museum. However, it was, after all, a gun, and at the time I was mightily pleased to have captured it.

On our march back to gain touch with the rest of the force, we came upon great stores of ammunition. The powder was packed in calfskins, very tightly compressed, and these I destroyed, though I had some difficulty with them on account of their solidity. I collected them into heaps, and I cut into one or two of them with my sword. Then, having spread the powder about, and made long trains of it, we tried to blow them up. Many of these skins were blown right up into the air, and yet came down again unexploded, though full of holes. With perseverance I managed eventually to destroy the lot, but it was such a long and tedious job that we did not get back to the camp until very late. There I reported to the General, and was duly complimented.

During our march from Tientsin to Pekin, another attempt to make peace was made by the Chinese Government. Early one morning three mandarins came into our camp, and declared that they were empowered to treat with us. At this time I may say that all we subalterns were afraid that we should not be allowed to go to Pekin, and I think that Lord Elgin, our Plenipotentiary, had arranged with the mandarins that only

## THE INDIAN MUTINY

a very small force—merely as a display—should ride through the streets of Pekin.

This conference with the mandarins lasted for a long time, and while it was going on, Parkes and Loch, who were on Lord Elgin's staff, with a score of men of the K.D.G. and about fifty of our native cavalry, strolled into the Chinese camp. Their idea was that they would be unmolested, but they had scarcely got inside the camp when all of them were taken prisoners; and at the same time the high mandarins rode away, and any number of concealed guns opened upon us.

At that moment we were having breakfast in a field of Indian corn, which had just been cut and was in shocks, and as soon as the guns sounded, and a round shot or two had come close to us, I jumped up and shouted, "Hurrah, for Pekin!" We fell in at once, formed line, and our artillery opened upon them. The results were that we took their guns and drove them off the field. But, by treachery, they had got some seventy prisoners, and these men were all more or less tortured, and most of them died. Their wrists and ankles were tied very tightly together with strips of raw hide, and they were then strung by their ankles and wrists on bamboos, and carried about the country.

It was known that they were taken to Yuen Min Yuen, and flung down before the Emperor.

Parkes and Loch fared better. They were, we heard, imprisoned near the Antin Gate in Pekin; and Parkes, who knew the language, met a mandarin whom he had known in Canton, and who stood his friend.

Continuing our march to Pekin, I again found myself on the advance guard, which consisted of a battery of R.A., a wing of 2nd Queen's, and my wing. We had just arrived at our camping-ground, and the R.A. were busily engaged with a flock of ducks, of which there were some two thousand swimming about on a canal close to us. I had also sent our messman to get a few ducks. Suddenly two guns opened fire upon us from the other side of the canal. I at once ran to General Michell, who had come up, to ask him to allow me to take these guns, and I obtained his consent. The next minute I saw Major James, of the 2nd Queen's, coming up, and I felt sure that he was on the same errand. So I begged the General not to allow him to take the command from me, and was told that James should be given orders to follow in reserve.

Several large boats were on the canal, and by a little management I got two of them

## THE INDIAN MUTINY

held together by the ends, and these were long enough to enable my four companies to cross. Then I kicked the boats apart, because I was not anxious for the major to be too near me. We formed line on open ground and, advancing immediately, we soon saw some 3000 men lining the wooded bank of a small winding brook, with a considerable village in the centre of the position. The enemy were armed with matchlocks, so I ordered my men not to fire until they were quite close.

I had seen the Chinese method of loading their matchlocks. After putting in the powder, they jarred the butt on the ground and then dropped the ball in. I never saw any of them use a ramrod, though I believe they had one. Consequently they were bound to fire in the air, or the bullet must have fallen out.

The result was as I had anticipated. When we were fifty yards away, they fired a volley at us without hitting one of my men, though Major James, who was some distance behind, had three men wounded. Then we charged with the bayonet and accounted for a few, but most of the enemy ran for the village—which we took—and streamed out at the back. In this village Sotheby had a hand-to-hand fight with an enormous Tartar, but one of our men came up at an opportune moment and killed the giant.

While the men were re-forming line on the plain, I saw a group of eight Tartars who obviously meant to show fight. To these I rode, and was at once set upon by the lot. I soon saw that although all of these men were armed with matchlocks, only two of them had loaded weapons. My charger was an extremely handy animal, and by twisting him this way and that way and directing my attention solely to the men with loaded matchlocks, I at length got a fair cut down upon the head of one of them, and almost in the same second I pulled my left rein and ran the other loaded man through the chest. My syce, who, armed with a very sharp tulwar, came up at this moment, settled another man, and then the rest of them ran away. For days afterwards my horse and I suffered from the bruises which we received from the empty matchlocks.

Immediately after this I was aware of a troop of cavalry in single rank, and with their commanding officer, in a yellow satin jacket, in the centre. I was, of course, the only mounted man on our side, but I did not see that this was a reason for allowing these fellows to go off calmly at a walk. So, putting spurs to my horse, I rode for the left side of the yellow satin jacket, and going through the troop at a gallop, I gave the commanding officer a backhander in the face as I passed. At the same time I dropped my reins and pressed my revolver to the back of my left-hand man. One of the bullets, however, had slipped, and the chamber would not revolve, so he escaped.

As soon as I had got through the troop they naturally pursued me, but my horse was faster than any of theirs, and in a few minutes I found myself cantering ahead quite easily. Then swinging around to the left I rejoined my men.

Marching on, we came across five camps of the enemy, and we took large quantities of ammunition and many standards, but all the guns had been moved off. By this time our General was getting nervous about our long absence from the main body, and orderly after orderly came up ordering me to return. To each of them I pointed out that it was necessary to advance a little farther, so that we might take this or that camp. When we had reached the last camp and could find no more opposition, I formed fours and marched back by the way we had come.

The Commander-in-Chief sent for me

when I had returned, and I reported to him what we had done. In reply he said, "I think it will be better for you to make a report of the whole thing." Of course I consented, for I thought it a great honour, but it would have been very much better for me if he had made the report. As it was, I never appeared in despatches, and as for my report—who cares for a lieutenant's report? Without doubt it was promptly burked.

# CHAPTER XII

Peace and prisoners : The shops of Pekin : A French officer and his loot : A wonderful watch : Bargaining with the Frenchman : Pearls of small and great price

WE had no more fighting, but as we approached Pekin, on some grass downs to the north of it, I was able to secure a flock of 1200 sheep. Keeping a few for our own use, I handed over the rest to the commissariat, and was again complimented by the General.

The walls of Pekin were very high and massive; so broad, indeed, at the top that three carriages might be driven abreast upon them. The gates were strongly defended, and there were very large towers on the walls. We encamped at quite a short distance to the north of the Antin Gate, for the Chinese did not seem to have any guns mounted upon the walls. The day after our arrival we had two or three batteries in position only 200 yards from the walls. And the question was whether these field-guns could make a breach in such a solid mass.

The Chinese, however, were again begging for a truce, and by this time they were honestly anxious to make peace. The first thing demanded by us was that all the prisoners should be given up. This they conceded as far as they could; but a great many of our men were dead, and those who were brought in were terribly maimed and altogether in a most shameful state, their wrists and ankles being full of maggots.

We had reason to feel indignant, and it was proposed to demand compensation from the Chinese Government. I do not precisely know the amount of this, but I remember to have heard that £10,000 was to be demanded for every native, and £100,000 for every European. Of this, I think, Lord Elgin did not see the justice, and he was reported to have said that if these terms were insisted upon the burden would fall upon the people alone, whereas these prisoners had been flung before the Emperor himself, who ought also to be made to suffer. Accordingly some moderate compensation was demanded, and Lord Elgin determined to burn the Emperor's summer palace of Yuen Min Yuen to the ground. In the meantime, officers were allowed to go into Pekin in pairs, never singly, and in uniform and fully armed.

Pekin was an especially dirty place, with broad streets, but covered with black filth. It appeared to be the custom of the Chinese

## THE INDIAN MUTINY

to throw anything they did not want into the streets, and there were no sanitary arrangements of any kind.

There were two cities, the Chinese city and the Tartar city, and in the southern one we found some capital shops. The butchers' shops contained rats and dogs hanging by their tails, beautifully clean to look at, and skewered just as our butchers hang up their mutton. I do not think that any of us were bold enough to test these dainties, and in fact my lunch was always made off sweetmeats, which were truly excellent. In Pekin I saw for the first time walnuts preserved in white sugar, and all sorts of preserved fruits were extremely common and good.

The people seemed to be quite friendly, and never interfered with us. I inspected various temples, notably the Temple of Heaven. In the northern city was the great palace of the Emperor, called "The Forbidden City," but we were not allowed to visit that.

Sotheby, young Elton, and I, however, made several expeditions to temples and palaces in the neighbourhood; and on one of these expeditions we discovered the great bell of Pekin in the courtyard of a monastery, about three miles to the north of the city. It has been said to be the largest bell in the world. There was no clapper, and it was struck on the edge by a solid log of hard wood, and the sound produced was most beautifully mellow and harmonious.

About this time I found myself in request as a valuer of various precious stones, &c. Several of our fellows had made purchases, principally of gold and pearls, from the French, and most of these were brought to me for my opinion of their worth. Our General, too, constantly asked me to breakfast, and afterwards to go to the French camp with him to see what we could buy. We were most successful, especially in the matter of pearls, which seemed to be regarded by the French as of no value. Except in watches, there seemed to be no diamonds.

The French had now withdrawn from the Summer Palace, and were encamped close to us. So one afternoon Sotheby, Elton, and I went for a walk through their camp, and saw an officer with a box before him in front of his tent, and showing what was evidently his loot to an admiring circle of friends. We were looking on at a respectful distance, when he came forward and asked us if we would like to see his " little collection of curiosities."

Of course we were delighted to do so. There were ten of us altogether, counting

## THE INDIAN MUTINY

French and English, and they found us empty vermuth boxes to sit upon. The fortunate owner of the box (which was really an old tea-chest such as hold 100 lb. of tea) was a Captain of Infantry in the Marines, and he was also the happy possessor of a remarkable watch, which I will describe.

It was round in shape, about the size of a tennis-ball. The case was literally a hollow sphere of the finest rose diamonds set in open gold, seventy-six of them altogether, the largest one being nearly three-quarters of an inch in diameter. One side of this sphere was open sufficiently to disclose the face of the watch, and the case was arranged to open so as to permit of the removal of the watch by means of a small key or handle about half an inch long on one side.

The makers' name was Clarke and Dunster, and it had Charles I.'s cipher on the key.

Such a watch was, I take it, absolutely unique.

The treasures enclosed in the box were marvellous, and must, I should think, have been worth quite £100,000. Two necklaces, exactly alike, of very large pearls especially attracted my fancy. Eighteen pearls went round the neck, and there were twenty-three in all, the remaining five in each case being in pendants in front.

With the box in our midst we all sat round, and everything was handed about for our inspection. This lasted for an hour, and then the jewels were returned, and one of the little group, a senior French officer, on getting up to go, remarked, "I congratulate you, Captain; it is a very nice box, and must be worth, I should think, quite 30,000 francs."

This gave me an idea, and as I shook hands with the Captain and thanked him for his kindness, I added, "Your friend thinks your box is worth 30,000 francs. I shall be happy to give you that amount for it."

He, however, assured me that a French officer merely collected these things "pour l'honneur et pour la gloire," and would never dream of selling them. "Yes, yes, quite so," I replied somewhat impatiently, "but all the same, should you happen to change your mind you will let me know?" and so I wished him good-bye.

I could not help thinking about that box, and the tip that had been given me as to its estimated worth. So I reconnoitred the French camp the next day without seeing anything of my Captain of Marines, but on the following day I was there again, and he, spying me out when I was quite a long way off, came up and asked me to come and have a liqueur. Then he took me to his tent, and, having given me a glass of vermuth, said, "Monsieur, I will take your offer." "What," I said, "the 30,000 francs for the box? Let me have a look at it," and he ordered his servant to bring it in. I at once said that more than half the things were gone, and I told him so. Whereupon he asked me if I doubted his honour, and I answered that I knew nothing about his honour, but that he must remember two necklaces of pearls, with twenty-three pearls in each necklace, and that they had gone. This he could not contradict, so I went on to tell him that I had set great store by those pearls, because I had wanted to give them to the lady to whom I was engaged to be married. He then began rather to sneer at my professed knowledge of pearls, and as things were getting unpleasantly warm I changed my tactics and said, "I will tell you what I will do. I will choose the pearls I want from your box, and then you shall fix the price. Will that suit you?"

To this, although he was rather angry, he consented, for I am sure that he considered me a complete duffer.

I chose seventy-eight pearls of all sizes

from the box, none of which, I should say, were worth less than ten pounds apiece, and a great many of them must have been worth from £100 to £250 each. "How much for the lot?" I asked, and was told that he must have £50 English money for them. "It is a great sum," I said, but after some little hesitation I agreed to give it to him.

At this moment out of a bit of old rag there dropped the finest pearl of all; it was the size and shape of a pigeon's egg, and of a most perfect lustre. "You will give me that in," I said to him. But he replied that he expected five English pounds for it, and eventually I gave him £55 for the lot. I may say now that when I returned to India I was offered 6000 rupees for this splendid pearl, but at the time I bought it there is no doubt that this Captain imagined that I was buying something of no value whatever.

As soon as the transaction was complete, the Captain left me in the tent with his soldier servant, and I could hear him laughing in the next tent with his brother officers and chuckling over the way in which he had "stuck" the Britisher.

The servant, who spoke broken English, immediately assured me that I had been nicely taken in. And when I asked him what he meant, he answered, "There is not

## THE INDIAN MUTINY

one of those pearls that you have bought that is worth a franc. All my life I have been working in pearls. I come from a place on the Seine, below Paris, where we made them in thousands." (I recognised the name at the time as being famous for the manufacture of false pearls, but I have since forgotten it.) " In your regiment, then, I daresay you have many more?" I queried. "Oh, yes, they are in huge numbers. I will show you." And I agreed that he should take me to see them as soon as I had settled with his master.

Soon afterwards the Captain returned in the most cheerful spirits, and I offered him £200 for his watch, but he asked £250 for it. "No," I told him, "I am a man of my word. I will give you £200." Then I asked him if I might take it away with me, and remove the centre diamond and weigh it. And to this request he replied, "By all means, if you will replace it."

I had that watch in my possession for some weeks, and took out the diamond, weighed it, and put it back again. I always intended to have the watch, but one day, as ill-luck would have it, I met the soldier servant close to my own tent, and giving him the watch I said, "Tell your Captain I still stick to my offer of £200." The next day the French marched away, and I have

# REMINISCENCES

never seen either the Captain or his watch since.

Now to return to the subject of pearls. One day the soldier took me to his lines and sent for the men who had pearls. These fellows brought me any number of false ones, which I said were magnificent, but not at all what I wanted. At length two old soldiers came along and sat down on the ground by me. Then out of some rag they pulled four first-rate pearls, the size of large marrowfat peas and perfect in every way. For these they asked four piastres (dollars). Just as I was concluding this bargain a fifth pearl popped out from a fragment of rag. I said, " I will take that one also," and was told that I could have it in with the rest. So I got five pearls for four dollars. They were worth 250 guineas apiece !

## CHAPTER XIII

*On a looting expedition : Another watch : Baskets of loot : The prize fund : Burning the palace : Gold, and my way of securing it*

IN the evening after our arrival at Pekin we heard that our cavalry had reached the palace of Yuen Min Yuen, but as it was a walled place they were not allowed to enter it. The French infantry, who were with our cavalry and had no such restrictions imposed upon them, were having the time of their lives.

The loot was immense, for nothing had been moved. The place had been left in charge of eunuchs only, who had shouted, "Don't commit sacrilege," and then run away. During that afternoon I was walking on the downs to the north of our camp and met Dick Harrison, who had been at Chilari Ghat with me. He had just returned from the French camp, and he told me of the loot, and, pointing out a pagoda some seven miles away, said, "If you ride for that pagoda you will find the French camp within a hundred yards of it. The whole camp is full of clocks, dozens and dozens of them ; watches, silks, satins, and everything you can imagine. I have never seen such a show."

News of all this came to Sir Hope Grant's ears, and during that night he very kindly issued a general order that half the officers of every regiment might go and loot. They had to return at noon, so that the other half might go. This suited me admirably as I was second in command, and I think that I may take some credit to myself for being only twenty minutes late in returning.

Of course, on the following morning I was up early, but the camp was up earlier still; and, as I was mounting my horse at the door of my tent, a procession of officers of all ranks, headed by the chaplain, passed me, bound for Yuen Min Yuen.

Galloping across country, I got to the pagoda a good hour before the procession arrived, and at once found the French camp, which was quite close to the south gate of the palace. The first thing I met was a country cart coming out of the gate, and escorted by French soldiers with fixed bayonets. It was full of gold in lumps which we called shoes, because they were cast somewhat in the shape of a shoe

There was a French guard at the gate, who saluted me. Across the courtyard was the great Hall of Audience, but everything, except some very large cloisonné vases, had been looted. I turned to the right into

## THE INDIAN MUTINY

a small room, which was full of yellow pamphlets. These were, I feel sure, catalogues of the contents of the palace.

While I was standing in this room, two French soldiers came in, and one of them was swinging something glittering in his hand. Then I asked him if he had "anything of curiosity" to show, and he replied, "I have nothing but a watch." In answer to my request to see it, he put into my hand a magnificent watch of blue enamel, with a sun of diamonds on the back, the centre stone of which was more than half an inch in diameter. Pearls, wonderfully matched, made a border, back and front. The makers' name was Barraud and Lund.

"I wish to buy," I told the soldier, and he asked me to fix a price. This, however, I declined to do, for I knew that I should spoil the bargain. But as he absolutely refused to name any sum, I at last suggested that his friend should fix the price. The friend immediately said, "Fifteen piastres," which meant fifteen dollars. But the owner of the watch was disappointed at this, and complained that some other man had got twenty-five piastres for his watch. "I'll give you twenty piastres," I said, and with this offer he was quite pleased.

Then I tore a blank sheet out of one of

the yellow catalogues, and wrote my name, rank, regiment, and IOU for twenty dollars, and he did not take the trouble to come for his money until more than a month had passed by. The watch, like everything else in the palace, had two small Chinese labels upon it, and some time after I showed them to Wade, our interpreter, and he read them for me. In this way I discovered that I owned the watch which had been presented by Lord McCartney to the Emperor in 1792. When I got back to England again I took this watch, with the chatelaine attached, to Barraud and Co., Cornhill, who told me that it had cost five hundred guineas.

Although at the time I did not know the actual value of my purchase, I was not inclined to think that I had made a bad start, and I wandered on through suites of rooms, most of which had been thoroughly looted. Nevertheless, I was able to pick up a few trifles. I got a square jade seal of the Emperor's, with the vermilion still in the stamp, which had been used for appointing governors and high mandarins to their posts; this seal had a carved handle, representing a sort of lion.

I also got a curiously shaped flower-pot made of gold wire, with letters of white coral worked in the wires. It had earth in it, from the centre of which there came a gold tree about a foot high, with turquoise fruit on it, and each fruit had a ruby centre. In addition, I obtained a great many rolls of silks and satins of the very best quality, and altogether I filled seven large baskets with loot of various kinds. Plenty of baskets were to be got from the guard at the gate, and the officer in charge offered me as many Tartar coolies (prisoners) as I required. I had tied my charger to an iron post at the gateway, and, having mounted him, I kept my seven Tartars, with their loads, in front of me, and rode back, revolver in hand, to camp at Pekin.

As I have already said, I was only twenty minutes late in returning. But when I found that my friend Keppel, who was to take my place, would not take the trouble to go, I wished that I had stayed longer, for I thought that the extra time could have been most profitably employed.

In the evening, when the order-book came round, we received a blow. Sir Hope Grant stated that, as the men could not be allowed to go to the palace and as the officers had already got such an astounding amount of loot, he intended to make a prize fund. For this purpose he had been able to obtain the sum of £20,000 from Montauban, the French General, and he went on to say that all the loot was to be sold by auction, and the proceeds were to be put into this fund. What, however, we had bought from the French we were to be allowed to keep.

When, some days afterwards, it had been decided that the palace should be destroyed, the First Division was ordered to march to Yuen Min Yuen. Accordingly we arrived there late one afternoon, and our orders were to enter the big gates at daylight the next morning, in detached companies, each company with an officer. Then we were to march as far as every company could in every direction, and having got as far as possible, we were to turn back to the gateway.

We had been recommended in general orders to loot all we could, and to take carts and bring back whatever we liked. Not being attached to any company, I was quite independent, and having a fair knowledge of topography, I started from the great southern gate with the fixed intention of going to the north. However, I could never get very far away, for I was always brought to a standstill either by a deep canal of clear water or by enormous walls of artificial rockwork.

It turned out that the palace covered eleven square miles, and really it gives a

## THE INDIAN MUTINY

wrong impression to call it a palace. It was a series of palaces, many of them connected together by corridors or passages, or with steps here and there, and with bridges over all sorts of places.

At last I got through into what seemed to be the private sitting-room of the Emperor. On the tables were various wonderfully carved lacquer boxes and cases of all descriptions. There were also some splendid carvings of scenery, and of these I helped myself to two and took them back to the gate. Then I again started to go north, and once more was brought up suddenly by a long, high blank wall. Leaning against this was a single plank, and being pretty active, I managed by crouching and getting my fingers under the sides of the plank to reach the top of the wall, and found myself looking down into a *cul-de-sac*, with a long, narrow passage.

The right side consisted solely of wall, but the left side had three doors in it, and I had come in at the blind end. My next adventure was to drop down and enter the first door, which opened into a courtyard, some 35 feet by 25. In the middle of the left side of the yard was a door, and on passing through it I found a large go-down, or chamber, with three six-feet deep shelves round the three sides of it. These had held articles of jade, and evidently this chamber had been a magazine of jade, but nothing had been left excepting some very large vessels and carvings which were almost too big to carry. However, I took one thing rather like a carved paving-stone.

Then I went out into the passage again, and, entering the second door, I found the same kind of courtyard, a similar go-down with the door in a similar place, three shelves round the sides and the two ends, precisely identical. This had evidently been a magazine of enamels, but only things so big that it was almost impossible to carry them remained. Here I took a big grotesque sort of demon with an open mouth, and going out into the passage again with my demon in one hand, I took up my paving-stone and came to the third door. Once more I found a precisely similar courtyard, but in this spot four or five Sikhs were engaged in chiselling off small pieces of what appeared to be two large broken pagodas. I lifted up the bell part of the largest pagoda, and having raised it about an inch off the ground, I knew immediately from the weight that it was gold. This pagoda had evidently been seven feet high, and the other about six inches less. They were in shape like the ordinary Bur-

# THE INDIAN MUTINY

mese pagoda, the lower third consisting of steps, then the large bell, and the spire rising from that. The spire was nearly solid, with Tibetan letters all around it in rings, and was very heavy. The steps also were very solid, and the bell part was about the thickness of a rupee.

I asked the Sikhs what they were doing, and one of them answered, "Breaking off bits to sell to the Europeans for gold." Then I went down into the go-down on the left, and found it of the usual size, with three shelves, from which everything had been taken. Fighting had taken place there, for bits of men's skulls were lying about, but their bodies had been removed. This had obviously been a magazine of gold ornaments of all sorts.

After inspecting the place I returned to the courtyard, and said to myself, "Here is a fortune on this bit of ground. How shall I manage to get it away?" My best plan, I thought, was to begin by assuming the airs of a languid swell, so I lounged against the outer entrance door, and seeing a man of the 60th Rifles at a little distance, I beckoned to him.

When he had come up I asked him his name, and whether he had been in luck. In reply he told me that he had not got anything, because he did not know what to take.

"Much my case," I said, "but I think of taking all this stuff, if there is anything in it. Will you help to carry it to the gate?"

"Certainly, sir," he answered, and was quite willing to have me decide upon a fair payment for his services.

As I was beginning to load him up with a portion of the pagoda I saw another man of his regiment, and soon arranged with him also to carry a load. Then I said to the Sikhs, "Come along, you fellows, take all this up. I am going to take it to the gateway."

I had now seven men well loaded, and had to pass through two large courtyards, where a hundred or more soldiers, R.A.'s and others, were kicking about the Imperial footstools of yellow embroidered satin, and playing a kind of rough football with them. I took care not to touch a bit of this gold myself, for I had the reputation in the camp of knowing the value of things, and I thought that if I was seen with any of my latest loot there would be a scrimmage, and that I should only get as much as I could carry myself.

Among the men whom I met was Lane Crawford's agent, who had accompanied the forces with all sorts of provisions and wines,

# THE INDIAN MUTINY

which he sold to the various messes, and bought any loot he could get in exchange.

"Are you taking all that rubbish? Why, it is only brass; I saw it this morning," he said.

"Oh, well," I answered, "perhaps I have not enough brass in my composition. Anyhow, I feel as if I want this."

We managed to get the gold eventually to my tent, where I wrapped it up in my blankets. The steps, however, of one pagoda were missing, and I saw them the next morning behind the cart of our Adjutant. So one of the Sikhs must have bolted and made his own bargain.

# CHAPTER XIV

I return to the palace and get more loot : Edmund Ward's story : A piece of bad luck

THIS gold was all of a very hard and very pale metal, and undoubtedly looked like brass. Almost everyone had seen it before I did, and had passed it by as worthless. Afterwards it turned out to be alloyed with eight per cent. of silver, but no copper, and it was worth about £22,000.

Having settled with my carriers to their satisfaction, I went to have a talk with "Jack" Randal, my C.O. It was now 2.30 P.M. and the force was waiting with piled arms for three companies of our regiment, under Edmund Ward, which were missing. At last I got tired of doing nothing and said to Randal, "If you don't mind I should like to have another look at that go-down from which I got the gold. It is only about 250 yards from here." "All right," he replied, "you will hear the bugles."

Thereupon I took my orderly, Gooditt Sing, with me, and found that the roof of the go-down was alight, as indeed were all the surrounding buildings. I could not, however, help thinking that, in a place

## THE INDIAN MUTINY

where such a lot of wealth had been, and in which there had quite evidently been a free fight, there must be something still left. The floor, I noticed, was paved with square tiles, and having taken a large nail from the wall and run it between the tiles, small broken pieces of gold and pearls at once began to spurt out. Goorditt Sing soon found another nail and also set to work. Before the roof began to fall in and we thought it was time to go, I had got two double handfuls of these fragments, and he nearly as much.

When we had returned there were still no signs of the missing companies, and everyone was becoming impatient. Then, about 4.30 P.M., when I was close to the gateway, I heard a voice saying, "Where's Harris?" and I saw Edmund Ward holding in his arms a large image of Buddha—the usual cross-legged image in the attitude of contemplation.

Directly I felt the weight of the image, I knew that it was gold and told him so. But he was not to be easily convinced; in fact, he was determined not to be.

"It is not gold, it can't be gold," he said, and then, by way of a change, he called himself "a d——d fool."

"My dear fellow, it is gold," I assured

him, but this only made him rave more than ever.

"If you don't believe it," I continued, "I'll give you £500 for it now. But I don't want you to take it, for you are a pal of mine, and your image is worth a lot more than that."

This, however, seemed to increase his fury so much that I asked what on earth was the matter with him.

"The matter!" he cried. "Why, I only brought one away, and I left 499 of them behind!"

Then he told me his story in the following words:

"Just after you left me at one o'clock I found a small door leading out of the Emperor's quarters, through which I got away north. All the grounds and buildings were absolutely untouched; neither the French, nor the Chinese coolies, had looted them at all. The scenery was very varied, and full of artificial effects. As you know, our orders were to go as far as we could, and then turn back to the gate. When I had gone about two miles, I thought that I had gone as far as it was prudent to go, and seeing a very large and fine temple on a hill, with a lake below and a lot of marble staircases and a bridge, I considered that

## THE INDIAN MUTINY

this would be a good place to begin upon. On entering the temple I saw a colossal statue of Buddha at the farther end, and all round the hall on tiers, like plants in a hot-house, were five hundred of these gods."

Here I may say that I knew he was right about the number and was not exaggerating, for it was quite usual in Buddhist temples to have an image for each one of the five hundred attributes of Buddha.

" While the men were lighting up," Ward continued, " I amused myself by cutting and slashing these images. Having broken my sword, as you remember, in one of the earlier actions, I was armed with a native tulwar. I cut off the ear of one image, and taking it up I thought it was very heavy and must be gold. Then I handed it to Subahdar Nutha Sing, who immediately said, 'Sahib, yih sonar hai' ('This is gold'). I cut another image in the same way, and it was evident they were all alike. This made Nutha Sing think, and presently he said, 'In what book was it ever written that there were five hundred gold gods of this size? It is impossible, but all the same give it to your orderly to carry.' And here it is."

So ended Ward's story, and while the bugles were sounding the "fall-in," I asked him how far away this temple was, and he answered, "About two miles." Thereupon I rushed off to interview the General, Sir John Michell, who had just mounted his horse, and with his staff around him was waiting for the troops to fall in.

"General, can I speak to you privately?" I asked, and as he at once drew away from the rest of his staff I continued: "I have come on a big thing. If you will leave me here with my wing I can be back at the Pekin camp by 11 o'clock or so." "What is it?" he asked, and when I had told him that it was gold in great quantities, he shook his head and replied that he could not give me leave.

"But, General," I ventured to expostulate, "such a chance as this will never come again; it is the chance of a lifetime!"

"I should have been delighted to help you," he returned, "but it is already 5 o'clock and getting dark, and we have got seven miles to march back to Pekin. I can't do it now, but I will tell you what I will do. At daybreak to-morrow morning I will send you out with your wing as a foraging party."

"That will be splendid," I said, "with all the day before me, we shall be back in time for dinner."

We got back to the camp at Pekin in

## THE INDIAN MUTINY

time for 8.30 mess, and, alas, during dinner, the order-book came round with orders to march down country at daylight.

Some days later Ward sold his image to a Jew sutler for £676, for he was always most comically afraid that it would turn into brass. Each one of these gods was really worth from £1000 to £1200.

I was very uneasy in my mind at having got so much gold, and I took the first opportunity on the line of march to ask for an interview with the Commander-in-Chief. It was immediately granted, and then I admitted that I had between £10,000 and £20,000 worth of gold, and asked if I might keep it. "Why, yes, you saw the orders?" was the answer. "Yes, sir," I said, "I saw the orders, but you may remember that I got a large amount of gold and valuables before, and had to give them up." "Oh, yes," the Commander-in-Chief replied, "I had to make a prize fund then. I will never make another as long as I live."

Then I saluted, and left him with my feelings considerably relieved.

## CHAPTER XV

Our march back to Tientsin : Gunboats and language : A terrific gale : An unsuccessful attempt to attract pirates : Turtle-fishing

THE date of my interview with the Commander-in-Chief was October 19, and the thermometer fell to four degrees below zero. We were all clad in beautiful furs and other warm clothing, but a bell-tent, even with three in it, is not at all suited to very low temperatures. We soon gave up marching in the early hours, and generally started about eleven o'clock and reached our camping ground between 2 and 3 P.M.

It was too cold to stand about, and as soon as the tents were pitched we all went to bed. By four o'clock our one hot meal was ready, and we ate it lying on the ground in our rugs. All our other meals were cold, and consisted of game of all sorts—Pallas' sand-grouse, which were very good indeed, geese and ducks. These with a sackful of boiled hams and chupatties formed our meals. The sacks, one of hams and one of birds, were always on the mess-cart, and on the line of march were usually close behind the column. Whenever there was a halt, the mere sight of these carts made us hungry.

## THE INDIAN MUTINY

There was a great deal of dust owing to the high winds, and the sacks were as black as coal, as indeed was the outside of all our provisions. That, however, was of little consequence, and, with a bit of newspaper for a plate and a pocket-knife, we managed to do very well. We got down to Tientsin without any particular mishaps, and then were ordered to go on board the gunboats.

I had at this time fifteen transport animals and three carts, and what to do with these was a puzzle. However, as I owed Lane Crawford and Co. a bill of ninety-five dollars, I let them have the whole lot for the amount of the bill, and I think that they made a jolly good bargain.

We only stayed two hours or so in Tientsin, and away we went in a gunboat down the Pei-ho, which was a narrow river with a very strong tide. Each of these gunboats, of which there were many, was commanded by a lieutenant, with a boatswain for his next officer.

I have already mentioned that the tone of the Navy in those days was different from that prevailing in the Army, and if I had not known this before, my journey down the Pei-ho would have convinced me of it. Steaming down the river at a good rate, we soon became aware that another gunboat was approaching, and I saw that our lieutenant was in a great state of mind. We pulled in as close to the bank as we could, so that the other gunboat might have room to pass, but nothing appeared to please the officer in command of the approaching boat, and he used the most foul, forcible, and scurrilous language.

They got by at length, and we pulled out from the bank to resume our journey. But presently we saw another boat, and the same thing occurred, only the officer in command of this boat was more of an artist in the way of abusive language.

Again we started, and again another gunboat hove in sight, but on this occasion I saw that things were different. Our lieutenant was now quite cheerful and used all the language himself, for the third boat was commanded by an officer junior to our man. We did not get down to the anchorage at Taku until 9 or 10 P.M. on a very dark night. We let go the anchor near one of Her Majesty's ships, and the noise of the chain through the hawse-hole produced the hail, "What ship is that?" from the look-out man.

Our man replied, and presently a voice said, "If you don't get your anchor up at once, and take your troops to the *Forerunner*, I'll put you under arrest."

## THE INDIAN MUTINY

To this our lieutenant replied, " Sir, I have not half an hour's coal on board," and then we heard the voice out of the dark saying, " I don't care a d———n. Up with your anchor, and get your troops on board their ship at once."

It was no easy job to find the *Forerunner* among a fleet of more than two hundred vessels, but our lieutenant succeeded in doing it. And we saw no more of our gunboat friends.

I think that it was on the next day that the P. & O. steamer *Bentinck*, with the rest of our regiment on board, took us in tow, and we steamed east for the mouth of the Gulf of Pe-chi-li. The cold was more intense than any I had known, and a strong north wind was blowing, which soon developed into a tremendous gale. Both hawsers were broken, and the *Bentinck* was swept from end to end, and all the horses and deck furniture were swept overboard. Without any delay we had to set what sail we could. The *Forerunner* was rather shorthanded, so I allowed the captain to have a hundred Sikhs " to pull his strings," as I called it. This was by no means pleasant work, for every rope was as hard as wire.

The southern half of the Gulf of Pe-chi-li is practically a bight of shallow water, which becomes more and more shallow the farther you drive south. The waves were enormous, and our great fear was that we should get into such shallow water that we should bump the bottom out of the ship on the mud. We tacked east and we tacked west, and at last we got a small slant of wind on our boat, and were able to scrape through the entrance. We passed through some islands without any knowledge of the depth of the channel, but we chanced it and managed to get through along the coast of Shantung. The conditions then began to improve, and we were able to make a little southing. We sailed close past the Island of Quelpart, which looked rather like the south coast of Ireland, and were soon able to make a true course for Hong Kong. Within twenty-four hours or less we had reached a beautifully mild climate.

In due course we reached Hong Kong, and there I sold my gold to a Chinaman. I also sent home by the P. & O. quite a fine selection of silks and satins to my fiancée.

From Hong Kong we set sail for Singapore, and as I had heard a report that Chinese pirates abounded along the coast of Tonquin, I persuaded the captain to make the vessel look as if she was more or less in distress, and to sail near the coast. I kept my men

## THE INDIAN MUTINY

under cover as much as possible, and hoped that some of these pirates might be induced to attack us. But unluckily none of them swallowed my bait, and we got down to Singapore without any particular adventure.

Singapore was very hot, and while we were there I lost my orderly, Goorditt Sing. He accidentally fell overboard, and as he had any amount of gold around him in belts and other contrivances he disappeared and was never seen again.

From Singapore we sailed for Calcutta in beautiful weather, for the most part calm and the very lightest of airs, up through the Bay of Bengal, through the Mergui Archipelago—a series of beautiful islands covered to the water's edge with verdure. Through the whole of February 1861 we went on progressing slowly and steadily.

During this time I, having a boat of four oars always at my disposal, turned turtle-fisher. I got our captain to send a hand up to the cross-trees to report " turtle " floating upon the water. When " turtle on the lee-bow " was reported, I said, " Lower my boat," and off we went, I lying down in the bow with my arm over the side. When we got within a hundred yards or so of a turtle it became necessary to discover which was his hinder end. So we sculled up to him silently and slowly with the two aft oars only, and when we reached him I caught hold of one hind-leg and held on. The men then came forward, and, having got a couple of oars under him, prised him up and hauled him in by his hind-legs. We gave him a piece of wood to bite, and as a turtle never lets go he became quite harmless. I caught four or five turtles nearly every day, and considered myself to be rather an expert at the sport. We kept the turtles in the boats, which had been filled with sea-water. I gave all of them to the captain, and he sold them to the hotels in Calcutta.

In the course of our voyage we sailed up the coast of the Andaman Islands, and passed through the channel between the middle island and the north island. I had a good look at Narcondam, a very peculiar-looking island named after a Dutch navigator. It is in shape like a Stilton cheese and has perpendicular sides, with 300 fathoms of water thirty yards from it.

## CHAPTER XVI

Long leave : My marriage and honeymoon : An amusing landlord :. Roulette at Baden-Baden : My luck : The Brazilian : Homburg : Married life : Reorganisation of the Indian Army : We go to Calcutta

WHEN we reached Calcutta the regiment was immediately sent up to Meerut, a very good station, and I applied for six months' leave to England on " urgent private affairs." Leave was refused, and I was particularly disgusted with this, as if I took more than six months' leave I should lose my appointment as second in command, and under the old rules of the East India Company I was, at that time, entitled to three years' leave. I had, however, been engaged to be married for five years, and I meant going ; so I booked my passage in a P. & O. steamer and sailed on April 10.

Taking this long leave was most unfortunate for me, as far as my military career was concerned. For not only did I lose my regiment, but in the following year, 1862, the whole army was reorganised and the Staff Corps formed ; and when I returned in January 1864, I found that I had been completely forgotten, and was practically a " waif and stray." I shall have more to say on this point when I relate what happened when I went back to India.

But, on the other hand, fortune smiled upon me when, on July 3, 1861, I made a most happy marriage. Indeed, I cannot think that any man had a happier married life than mine, whether with my first or my second wife, and I hope that even those who think that one ought not to speak publicly of such things will pardon me for expressing my gratitude for so much happiness.

I started home in the P. & O. steamer *Indus*, but as there was no canal at that time she only took us to Suez. From Alexandria to Marseilles we travelled on a fast paddle-steamer, and in the Gulf of Lyons we encountered a most furious gale. George Allen of the Pioneers, Dobbin, R.A., and I travelled together across France, and, going by Boulogne and Folkestone, we beat the mails to England.

I remember landing at Folkestone on Sunday, May 12, as the bells were ringing for afternoon service, and going straight to the Pavilion Hotel. On the next morning I woke early, and with the window wide open and the birds singing I felt sure I was the most fortunate man in the kingdom, and going to be married to the best girl. Not a soul was expecting me for another month,

## THE INDIAN MUTINY

for I had been careful to take everyone by surprise. I had lots of money, and three portmanteaux full of Indian, Indo-English, and Chinese jewellery, furs, silks, the Emperor's watch, embroidered petticoats, everything, in fact, that I had been collecting for five years. And then, in addition, I had a ton and a half of heavier things coming round the Cape in the *Forerunner*. Truly, I felt that the world was a very good place.

I sent a wire to my fiancée to say that I should be at Allesley for lunch at 1.30, and when her mother heard that I was coming she remarked, " How terrible ! We were going to have up the carpets to-morrow for spring-cleaning." But I am glad to know that there were others in that house who were not appalled by the thought that the " spring-cleaning " would be upset !

I stayed in the village for some days, and then had to go to London to get some clothes. I went to my club, the East Indian United Service, drew the winner of the Derby in the Club Sweepstakes, and returned to Warwickshire.

We were married, as I have said, on July 3, and arranged to travel on the Continent for our honeymoon. After waiting at Folkestone for a good crossing, we arrived in Paris, and stayed at an hotel, in which, I remember, the furniture was very grand to look at, and quite impossible to use. Our room was crammed with a variety of wardrobes, which contained any number of drawers capable of holding a book apiece, but which were absolutely useless for clothes and nearly everything else.

From Paris we went to Cologne, then down the Rhine to Basle, and from there to Lucerne, where we stayed a considerable time at the Schweitzerhof. From Lucerne we made several excursions, driving over the Brünig pass to Meiringen; and afterwards we took the steamer on the Lake of Brienz to Interlaken, where we stayed a long time at the Hôtel des Alpes, the landlord of which hotel amused us very much.

One day when I was complaining of the bad quality of the beef, he said, "What would you? In this country we milk the cow until she will milk no longer; we then put her into the plough until she can work no longer; and then we make her into beef for you English." A frank, if not altogether satisfactory, explanation.

From Interlaken we went to Lauterbrunnen, Mürren, and by the Wengern Alp to Grindelwald, when we began to think of our return. Gradually working our way

## THE INDIAN MUTINY

northwards through Thun and Berne, we came by easy stages to Baden-Baden, and there I made my first acquaintance with roulette. We stayed at the Hôtel d'Angleterre, quite close to the Kursaal, and I resolved that, as I was now a happy married man, I would not go in for any big risks.

Accordingly, I put £20 into a separate purse, and said to myself, "There you are, Jim, you can amuse yourself with that, but when it is gone you will get no more as long as you stay here." We went to the tables, my wife taking her work and sitting on a sofa near me, and in two days I had converted that £20 into £800. Then I said to her, "Money goes, but jewellery remains. There are some very nice shops here, and you can have what you like out of the winnings."

My wife had lived most of her life quietly in the country, and had not, I suppose, ever had such a free hand. Consequently, she only spent about £100, and I went on playing, and lost all that remained of the £800, and £5 of my original £20.

Reduced to £15, I still continued to play, and luck turned. People often say "Fortune smiled on us"; in my case she must simply have roared with laughter. It seemed as if I could not do wrong. Always remembering that the pull of the table was against me, I never stayed more than half an hour at a time.

My daily programme was something of this kind. I would go to the table when it opened at 11 A.M., stay my half-hour, win from £500 to £1000, and then go for a walk with my wife. After that we lunched, and about half-past two I used to have another turn with much the same result, and then we would go for a drive. After dinner I put in a third half-hour, and invariably found it profitable.

By this time I always played the maximum (£480) on the even chances, and sometimes I had an inspiration and felt sure that I knew what would turn up. This, however, was rare, though I remember one instance well. I was certain that "*Trente-six, rouge, pair, et passe*" would turn up, and told all my neighbours, who were constantly asking me to place their stakes for them because I was so lucky.

For myself, I had the maximum on red, and I recollect that I had a pile of double Fredericks, as high as they would stand, on the column. I counted them as three to a £5 note, and after the first few days I always played in them. Day after day I continued to win. My place at the table was always kept for me, and I found myself pointed to as the man "who always won." One afternoon I remember particularly, for, after winning a considerable stake, I backed the red for the maximum eleven times running. Then I stopped, thinking it could not come up again; but it came up thirteen times consecutively, and on this the head croupier turned to me and said, "Voilà, Monsieur, you would have broken the bank."

My wonderful luck continued for several more days, until, in fact, a Brazilian gentleman arrived and stood opposite to me on the other side of the table. I liked his face, but he appeared to be considering me rather closely, and I remember thinking him very strongly magnetic. He began by backing zero, and up it came. This was something quite new, for previously I had not been at all troubled by zero. From this time I could not win; zero came up twice in about five times, and shortly afterwards, having lost considerably, I left the table. I tried again the next day, but the Brazilian was there and I could do nothing but lose.

I had lost a lot in those two days, but was still well to the good. So I thought it was time to leave Baden-Baden, and as my wife was ready to move we went on to Homburg, which was very gay, with crowds of people and the Kursaal in full swing.

Again I put £20 into a separate purse, and on the first day turned it into £60. Whereupon I divided this sum into £20 for profit, £20 for my original stake, and the remaining £20 to do what we liked with. But fortune resented this elementary system of division, and I found myself continually struggling with a five-franc piece. I had, however, one rather remarkable inspiration; for as my wife and I were walking through the rooms one morning, the croupier spun the marble for the first time. I knew at once what was coming, and said, "Twenty-eight, black," to my wife. I tried to get out my purse in time, but was too late. If my experience had been as great as it was afterwards, I should have backed 28 by putting my purse on the number and saying, "La limite."

We stayed for a week in Homburg, and then went on to Cologne and Spa. At Spa, of course, I tried the tables, but with no success, and from there we went on to Brussels and so home, after a most delightfully happy three months.

After spending several enjoyable weeks with relations, I took a house for the winter in the Holly Walk at Leamington, and

# THE INDIAN MUTINY

became a member of the Bedford Street Club. During this time I speculated freely and successfully in Cornish and Devon mines. Altogether the years '61 and '62 were very fortunate and happy ones for me.

I do not, however, propose to weary my readers with a chronicle of all the small events of a quiet and contented married life. This book is not intended to be a biography, and is only meant to contain incidents and events which may, I trust, prove of interest to someone.

Now I must mention an event which, at any rate, was of considerable interest and importance to me. In 1862 Her Majesty took over the Government and Army of India, and all the officers of the Indian Army were given the choice of three options:

1st. To remain in their old regiment under its new name, serving when out of India on English pay.

My regiment became the 2nd Battalion of the 104th.

2nd. To remain on the cadre of the old regiment, with no reasonable chance of employment. This was called doing general duty.

3rd. The Staff Corps.

I elected for this last and was appointed

to it from the date of its formation in 1862.

By the end of '63 I had come nearly to the end of my finances, so I took passages in the P. & O. for my wife, her maid, and myself. We broke down in the Red Sea, and were five days at anchor off Jeddo, but we reached Calcutta by the first week of January '64.

## CHAPTER XVII

An unsatisfactory interview : A swindle : Kindness of the Viceroy : More interviews : Barrackpore : The great cyclone

HAVING reported my arrival, I interviewed the military paymaster, Colonel Martin, a most excellent officer and a very good fellow.

"You probably know," I said, "that I joined the Staff Corps in '62, and am now of rather more than fourteen years and six months' service, with more than four years of it on the staff. Now, I have never seen myself in general orders as Captain."

"That is all very well," he replied, "but the Department decrees that leave does not count for service as regards the four years on the staff."

"I have read the Staff Corps warrant very carefully," I said, "and it distinctly states that every officer shall be Captain when he has completed twelve years' service, four of which must have been on the staff. There is not a word about 'leave not counting' in the warrant. I am therefore due to receive the difference of pay between the rank of Captain and that of Lieutenant from June 27, 1861, to this date."

"I may perhaps agree with you," he admitted, "but at the same time I must obey the Departmental orders. I have also to give you some further disagreeable information, for as you are now in Calcutta you are on half batta, and your pay is only 181 rupees 12 annas per month."

"This is even a bigger swindle than the other," I said. "Why, the half batta order is one of the old East India Company's rules. How can it possibly apply to me, when I am in the Staff Corps?"

"I am afraid that is all the pay you will get," he replied, and his fears were only too well founded.

For it was all I did get until I was appointed to the Loodiana Sikhs at Dorunda, Chota Nagpur, in October of that year. Then the half batta stopped, but I never received Captain's pay until I was over sixteen years in the service. And I consider that this was one of the biggest swindles ever perpetrated by a Government. Eighteen months afterwards they gave me the back rank, but never the pay, and by that time the back rank was very little good, for I had been passed over.

What I ought to have done was to have sued the Government in the High Court. I must have gained my case, as anyone can

## THE INDIAN MUTINY

see if he will take the trouble to read over the Staff Corps warrant.

As it was, I found myself in Calcutta with my wife, a lady's maid, and very few rupees in my pocket. They allotted me quarters in the Rampart Barracks in Fort William, for which they made me pay a high rent. There was no furniture whatever in my quarters, and this I had to get.

My wife faced our difficulties most bravely, and we soon knew everybody in Calcutta. My old Colonel, now General Sir George Showers, commanded the division, and we went everywhere and received any amount of sympathy. Dinners, balls, picnics to the Botanical Gardens, and parties of all sorts made life very pleasant, for although we may be said to have had no money and my pay was infinitesimal, my wife had plenty of frocks and jewellery.

Just after we had settled down in our quarters, the new Viceroy, Lord Lawrence, arrived, and took up his abode at Government House. Within a few days he gave his first dinner party, to which we were asked, and as his staff were more or less new to the place and the work, the pairing off of the guests was not quite efficient. I found myself a free-lance, and therefore looked out for a seat as near as possible to

Lord Lawrence. He took in a Mrs. Bright, the wife, of course, of some high official, and I, seeing my opportunity, sat on the lady's other side.

During dinner Lord Lawrence began to explain to this lady how curious it seemed to him to come out to India as Viceroy. "When I was twelve years in the service," he said, "I was here in this town and only drawing 400 rupees a month. I was seriously thinking of going to Australia."

As soon as he had finished speaking I leant across and said, "My case, my lord, is much harder than yours; for I have been nearly fifteen years in the service and am only drawing 181 rupees 12 annas."

"What!" he exclaimed. "Why, you were at Delhi!"

"Yes," I said, and then he told me to come and see him on the following day, and assured me that he would give me any appointment in his gift for which I considered myself fit.

On the next morning I went first to interview the Civil Secretary, and he showed me a list of appointments, some of which, especially the political ones, were very good indeed.

"This," I said, "will do for me, I think," and I pointed to one of them.

## THE INDIAN MUTINY

"The trouble is," the Secretary replied, "that all these civil and political appointments require you to pass in honours in two languages and in a knowledge of Indian Law."

"Thank you," I said; "what else have you got?"

"Well," he answered, "all the Viceroy's appointments require something of the sort, but we are just going to make a new appointment. This is Deputy Superintendent of the Andaman Islands, and the pay is 600 rupees a month."

"That means, of course, in addition to one's pay as Staff Corps Lieutenant?" I asked.

"No, consolidated," was the reply, and I informed him that I was not going to gaol on 600 rupees a month consolidated.

I must here explain that in the Andaman Islands is the great convict establishment of India, as many as 15,000 prisoners at a time being kept there. The principal harbour is Port Blair, and the garrison consisted then of two companies of a European regiment from Rangoon.

The appointment of Superintendent was a very good one, and not made less so by the fact that he always had a small steamer at his disposal. There were several medical officers in residence, and it must have been an economical place to live in, for I never heard of any shops, and the amusements of so limited a society could not have been very expensive. I also heard that prisoners for life, especially murderers, made very good servants, and there was a large selection to choose from! None of these attractions, however, made me anxious to take my wife to the Andaman Islands.

Having failed with the Civil Secretary, I went across and interviewed the Military Secretary. But the Viceroy's military appointments were either in Central India, which meant five days' travelling in a palanquin to get there, or they were on the further side of the Indus, a frightful climate in the hot weather and about equally difficult to get to or from.

One of the best appointments vacant was second in command of a Punjab cavalry regiment at Dera Ghazi Khan, as bad a climate as could be found in India. Another —and overwhelming—drawback was that I should have been obliged to buy three chargers, an impossible thing for me to do at that time.

It has always been my luck to be on the best of terms with Viceroys, but Commanders-in-Chief have looked upon me with

## THE INDIAN MUTINY

a different eye. I thanked Lord Lawrence, and told him how very sorry I was not to find something that suited me. Then I wrote various applications to the Commander-in-Chief, which General Showers backed up with most strong recommendations; but the result of our efforts was exactly nothing.

Presently the second in command of a native regiment at Barrackpore fell vacant, and I applied for this, and the General appointed me temporarily, pending orders from headquarters. This regiment I found to be in a very queer state. They had just got a new commanding officer, and he had put every officer in the regiment under arrest, and almost all the rank and file were doing extra drill. I managed to get on very well with the commanding officer, but I was the only man who did. However, I did not have a long experience of him, for after a month I returned to Calcutta, the appointment having been filled up.

While we were at Barrackpore, the great cyclone of June 4, 1864, the worst that has ever been known, occurred. We had a very good bungalow, which we shared with a young fellow of the 52nd and his wife. It had just been done up, and looked both sound and strong. The bungalow had seventeen rooms, one of which, fortunately, had a flat roof. The rest was newly and well thatched.

The storm began at 9 A.M., and increased tremendously and alarmingly. A pillar of the verandah was blown down, and in less than a minute the whole roof was carried away. Not a vestige of it was to be seen. We had to get into the drawing-room, and there we barred the doors with boxes and everything we could find. After a little time I said that I would go and see if I could find quarters in some flat-roofed house for us, and I managed to get to the Grand Parade, on the edge of which were the artillery guns, limbers, &c., under a big corrugated iron roof.

The limbers and carts were blowing about all over the place, just like children's toys. The guns alone resisted the cyclone. All the stables, both R.A. and Lahore Light Horse, were blown down. Over a hundred horses were loose, and fighting on the Maidan. Even some of the men's barracks had been hurled to the ground. The telegraph wires, being twisted round trees which had been uprooted, made the roads quite impassable for any traffic. A river steamer, with two flats, anchored in the middle of the Hooghly, was sunk. Seventy

## THE INDIAN MUTINY

steamers and large sailing-ships were thrown up on the Mall in Calcutta; the place was simply covered with them. One might go on recounting the disasters caused by this cyclone for almost any length of time.

While I was out looking for a shelter for us, the air was full of great branches of trees, and the noise was terrific. I walked into the park to see if any of the Staff bungalows were available, but they were not. I could not keep on any road, but was blown here, there, and all over the place.

I stood for a few moments on the windward side, you may be sure, of a tall casuarina tree. The casuarina is an Australian tree of very hard wood, and carries no sail. The trunk is without a bough of any sort for 70 feet, and the tree has a feathery kind of head. I had my back to it, and thinking that I had heard a sharper noise than usual, I turned to look; and the tree, which is one of the toughest and strongest of trees, had gone right away at a yard from the ground.

I got back to the remains of our bungalow feeling as if my breast-bone had been blown against my spine. Tons of bricks had fallen on our beds, and the place was quite uninhabitable. A great many natives had been killed, but, as far as I heard, no Europeans.

# REMINISCENCES

The behaviour of the birds was very curious; they were all on the ground, collected behind walls, and as I walked by them perhaps one or two would get up. These, directly they spread their wings, were flattened against the walls. The crows seemed to suffer the most damage.

Very soon I had to go out to try again for a place to shelter ourselves. I knew most of the people in the station, but my hopes rested mainly upon Colonel Swinhoe's house, which had a flat roof, and when I found the Colonel and his wife they very cordially agreed to take us in. By about 6 P.M. the cyclone had moderated, and after a great deal of difficulty, and with the help of my orderly, we eventually got the ladies to places of safety and comfort.

Some time passed before the road to Calcutta was cleared, but large fatigue parties of troops worked at it daily, and in a few days we were able to get back to our quarters in Fort William.

## CHAPTER XVIII

At Dorunda : G. : March to Ferozepore : Quarrels and plain speaking : I am put under arrest : But in spite of this am appointed Acting Magistrate : I offer to go to Abyssinia : Moradabad

DURING these impecunious days I could not, of course, help getting into debt, but I think that 1200 rupees were the extent of my liabilities, and I do not consider that this showed very bad management. We were fortunate enough to get my wife's maid well married to a large shopkeeper, and we were very glad that she was able to do so well for herself, since we were not in a position to do much for her.

At length, some time in October, I was appointed wing officer of the 15th Loodiana Sikhs. All numbers of regiments had been changed at the reorganisation in '62, and this was not the 15th I had formerly belonged to.

It was a first-rate regiment and was commanded by a first-rate man, Lieut.-Colonel R. Barter, and under his command we considered ourselves to be very well off. Hal Fellowes was second in command, and he became my greatest friend. Never was there a better fellow. We became inseparables, and I was truly sorry when he left (through getting a better appointment), even though I felt fairly certain that I should succeed to his post. Barter, indeed, strongly recommended me for it, but as usual the chief thought otherwise, and put in a man, to whom I will merely refer as G., over my head.

Dorunda was a capital station with a remarkably cool climate, being about 2200 feet above the level of the sea, and after Calcutta it seemed like Paradise. The civil station of Ranchi was about a mile off, and the Commissioner, Colonel Dalton, had a very fine house, with beautiful gardens, between the civil and military stations. Croquet was the fashion, and we had several capital matches, Military *v.* Civil. In fact we all pulled well together.

And then G. arrived and things began to change. For myself I can say that in a long life I have found it perfectly easy to get on with nearly every man, but I could not get on with G. My dog Peter was of the same opinion as I was, and went for G. whenever he saw him.

The natives said of this man that he was always riding either an elephant or a donkey, and they are generally right about their officers. One day he would fawn upon me, and I have known him to come into my

## THE INDIAN MUTINY

room, when I was suffering from neuralgia, and kneeling down by the side of my bed try to kiss my hand. But on most days he was just ordinarily disagreeable, and I liked him better—if I can possibly be said to have liked him at all—when he was intentionally unpleasant.

We stayed in Dorunda for two years, and in October '66 were ordered to march to Ferozepore, a distance of over a thousand miles. If G. had not been present this march would have been quite delightful. Most of the officers were present, and so Dick Barter allowed all the ladies to be honorary members of the mess.

Our course for almost the whole march was on the Grand Trunk road through Gya, Allahabad, Delhi, Umballa, &c. Barter had formerly been in the 75th Foot, and so we had been on the Ridge together in '57. We spent a most interesting day in taking our wives over the battlefield.

We arrived in Ferozepore in March. It is one of the hottest stations in India, but it has a very pleasant cold-weather season, which lasts until the crops are cut about the end of March. In April I got short leave, and took my wife up to the hill station of Dalhousie, where we hired a small bungalow. But when I returned to Ferozepore I found the weather frightful; even at midnight in the coolest house in the place the thermometer stood at 110°.

By the middle of October, when the ladies had come down from the hills, the climate was almost perfect. Nothing particular happened, but we had the usual parades and some amusements, including Umballa races. On St. George's Day the 5th Fusiliers marched in, and gave us great entertainment.

G. and I were still antagonists, and we had many small rows, without, however, arriving at an open quarrel. But after we had been inspected by General Rainier, commanding the Lahore Division, and given great satisfaction to him, Barter took leave to the hills. This left G. in command of the regiment, though only for ten days, as Barter, meaning to take his long leave later on, intended to—and did—return after that time.

I was made President of the Mess, in succession to G., and finding a large deficit in the accounts I did not mince matters, but said what I thought of him, which happened to be that I considered him a swindler. Of this candid opinion he, however, took no notice. All of us were without our wives at the time, and G. was chumming with a Major Rowlands, of the 5th Fusiliers.

## THE INDIAN MUTINY

When he told the story to Rowlands the latter asked what he had done about it. G. confessed that he had done nothing. "Of course, you ought to have put him under arrest. Do you mean to say you have not done so?" Rowlands asked.

During the next day the Adjutant came for my sword, and told me that I was under arrest. As I declared that what I had stated was the truth and that nothing would induce me to apologise, a Court of Inquiry was ordered by the Commander-in-Chief, and I remained under arrest for several weeks.

During this time, when the cantonment magistrate had taken leave, to my great astonishment I was made acting magistrate, and I carried on the work of the office until he returned at the end of the two months. As I was thus appointed to another post, it was clear that any fault I might have committed had been condoned. But I knew that I had done a very foolish thing in choosing a time when G. was in command of the regiment, and I began to think that my military career might possibly have come to an end.

The Abyssinian Campaign was then on, and I wrote to the Punjab Government offering to raise a regiment of a thousand Sikhs, and to take them to Abyssinia. They wrote back to say that they did not want any men, as they had already raised 1700, but that they would be glad if I would take them to Abyssinia.

In the meantime they had written to the General commanding the Lahore Division to ask what manner of man was this Lieutenant Harris, who had offered to raise a regiment of Sikhs. The General replied that he considered Lieutenant Harris to be one of the best officers in his division, and that if the Punjab Government could obtain his services they might consider themselves very fortunate.

The Commander-in-Chief was then Sir William Mansfield, a man I had never met. His orders upon the Court of Inquiry were that Captain G. should pay up the money found to be missing, as the deficiency might be due solely to his carelessness; that my conduct amounted almost to insubordination; and that I was to be sent to do general duty at Lahore.

Lahore was only fifty miles away, and there my wife and I took a small house in the cantonment. On my arrival I went to interview Colonel Black, Military Secretary to the Punjab Government, and I told him that I had not heard anything more about the 1700 Sikhs.

"That," he said, "will be all right. You

# THE INDIAN MUTINY

are to have the highest staff allowance that we can give, 400 rupees a month." And then he added that he would wire at once to the Imperial Government for my services, and that I should start some time during the following week. He also told me that the General had reported very highly upon me.

On the following morning I received two letters. One was the answer from the Imperial Government: "Lieutenant Harris having been removed from the 15th Sikhs for misconduct, his services are not available." The other letter was from the Commander-in-Chief, who said that he considered that in my case there were extenuating circumstances, and that he had much pleasure in offering me the appointment of station staff at Moradabad.

My wife and I held a council over these letters. I knew that I had only to call on Colonel Black and show him the Commander-in-Chief's letter; and that he would then apply again to the Imperial Government, and that I should almost certainly get the Abyssinian appointment. This would probably mean that my wife and I would have to part, and that she must go home to England—an expensive journey—with the added burden of having afterwards to keep up two separate establishments.

# REMINISCENCES

On the other hand, although the pay was small, Moradabad was a very good climate, only 70 miles from the hill station of Nynee Tal, and it was easy to get there. Eventually we elected to go to Moradabad.

I must add that when we left Ferozepore we had a great send-off, almost all the station coming to say good-bye and wish us good luck. I remember saying that G. would be in Lahore Gaol before six months had passed, and I have never made a truer prophecy. Within three months he was there for a dreadful crime. In fact, the case was so frightful that it was never tried, and G. was removed quietly from the Army, without court-martial, "Her Majesty having no further occasion for his services."

Some of my readers may be disposed to think that it would have been wiser not to have mentioned G. at all, but he had a very great effect on my life and prospects, and I had to account for my removal from my regiment. Also I wished to show that I am not naturally quarrelsome, and that I was justified in my opinion of this man.

## CHAPTER XIX

Butterfly : The Meerut Tent Club : A chronicle : A picnic worth remembering

WE had an easy journey to Moradabad, and before starting I bought at Lahore Races a very handsome country-bred mare, called Butterfly, which had been cast from the Government stud as barren. She was seventh in descent from Eclipse, and was the nucleus of my racing stable. Indeed, she proved to be a splendid bargain, for I won seventeen races with her.

Moradabad was a very pleasant place, with a good race-course and racquet court. It was also a civil station, and the terminus of the Scinde, Punjab, and Delhi railway. The garrison was only a regiment of native infantry and a wing of a European regiment.

Late in April my wife went up to Nynee Tal, and I used frequently to get ten days' leave and ride up, starting early, and getting there in time for dinner. This, in the rains, became rather an awkward job, for I had to cross two considerable rivers in flood, but Butterfly evinced a talent for swimming, and thoroughly enjoyed herself.

The cold weather of '66–'67 was most enjoyable, and among other pleasing events we were invited to a meeting of the Meerut Tent Club, for the Kadir Cup. This took place only 46 miles away, and so we drove to the bridge over the Ganges at Gurmucktesur, where our friend sent an elephant to meet us. On this visit I had my first experience of pig-sticking, and enjoyed it thoroughly. It is, I think, the best sport in the world. Mellor, of the Civil Service, provided us with tents and everything, and we spent a most excellent five days with the Tent Club. That year there were, if I remember rightly, thirty-two entries for the Cup, and Tom Studdy of the Artillery was the winner.

While looking over the records of this club someone discovered the following chronicle, and had fifty copies of it printed. One of these was given to me, and although the chronicle must be known to some of my readers, I venture to think that it will bear repetition. It is an account of the origin of the Kadir Cup.

" Taken from the records of the Meerut Tent Club.

" Translation of part of a cuneiform inscription found at Germ-ok-taza, supposed to be a portion of the Book of Spawt.

" And it came to pass in those days that Fawben[1] was a ruler in the land, and

[1] Forbes, the magistrate and collector of Meerut.

## THE INDIAN MUTINY

collected taxes for the king and administered justice to the people. And a great cry arose throughout the land from Delhi even unto Port,[1] and the people came unto Fawben saying: 'We are mightily oppressed by the unclean beast, and our bellies cleave unto the ground through fear of him, for he hath increased and multiplied exceedingly, and trampleth down our vineyards and devoureth our corn, and no man can stand before him. Come now and help us, or we shall die, we and our little ones.' And when Fawben heard this he was sore troubled, and called to Hill[2] the scribe, and Hill the scribe, having girded up his loins, came and stood and bowed before Fawben. And Fawben said unto him, 'Write now unto my young men, and say unto them, "Why tarry ye in your tents whilst the unclean beast vexeth the land? Are your spears rusty or your horses lame? Ye are called mighty hunters, but your mothers know not that ye are out, and ye tarry amongst your womenfolk that they may cherish your poor feet. Give them now your garments and take ye theirs, that they may come out and slay the unclean beast."' And Hill the scribe wrote as Fawben commanded him. Then great

[1] One of the meets of the Tent Club.
[2] Hill, the assistant magistrate.

shame fell upon the young men, and they smote their breasts and rent their garments, so that the tailors rejoiced, and they said among themselves, 'Woe to us because of this thing. Verily our faces are blackened this day.' And Fawben wrote again to the young men, saying, 'Come now out unto me, all ye that may, and bring your spears and your horses, even the best that ye have, and we will purge the land of the unclean beast, even the soor,[1] and slay him from the rising of the sun to the going down of the same, that the people may have rest.' And when the young men heard this their hearts were glad, and they made haste to do as Fawben had said. And there gathered together a great company to Shirpur, from the east and from the west and from the north and from the south, riding furiously upon one-horse chariots. Of the tribe of Topkhana[2] came Adg[3] that dwelleth upon the hill of ravens, and Hazligg and Robos[4] the mighty rider, and Bish[5] the son of the high priest; and of the tribe of Hooza[6] came Mulvil, the clerk, and Bedol,[7] that owned the swift horses, and Barrur[8] the beloved of

---

[1] Pig.   [2] Artillery.   [3] Ravenshill, Adjutant R.A.
[4] Hazlerigg and Roberts.
[5] Philpotts, son of the Bishop of Exeter.   [6] Hussars.
[7] Biddulph.   [8] Barrow.

# THE INDIAN MUTINY

women, whose head is like the sun, and Weester[1] the hairy man, and Dirzee[2] and many others; and Taffy[3] the centurion of the spearmen, from the land where the people eat cheese roasted with fire; Hamilt the treasurer and Saptum[4] the wise judge, and some of the tribe of Buff,[5] the men that are clothed in scarlet, all of them desirable young men. And Fawben erected tabernacles for the young men, and gave them to eat and to drink as much as they would, for they were exceeding thirsty.

"And Fawben gathered together a great multitude of the tribe of Hind, hewers of wood and drawers of water, and they took staves and instruments of music and smote the bushes and shouted greatly, so that the heart of the unclean beast became as water, and he fled before them. And the young men, having bound prickles on to their feet, pursued the unclean beast and smote him in the hinder parts and covered him with shame; and they strove greatly with one another who should first smite him with the spear, and they slew many, riding valiantly. And divers of the unclean beasts, being possessed with a devil, turned upon the young

---

[1] Webster.    [2] Taylor.    [3] Eardley Wilmot.
[4] Sapte, C.S.    [5] The Buffs.

men and sought to rend them with their tusks, and wounded many of their horses grievously ; but for such the young men stayed not their hands, nor did they cease to smite them till they had destroyed them utterly.

"And Barrur, whose head is as the sun, smote one of the unclean beasts, and his spear was loosed from his hand and his horse fell upon the edge of the spear so that he died : and men grieved greatly for the good horse and for the man, though the latter died not.

"And as the young men returned from hunting, there came one to meet them, riding furiously ; and when he came close to them they saw that it was Hill the scribe. And they asked him, 'Whence comest thou ?' And he answered and said, 'I am come from riding the beast Behemoth in the land beyond Gusy, where I have slain many wild beasts, and now I am come to help ye cleanse the land of the unclean animal,' and they said to him, 'Go to, where now is thy brother scribe, he that rideth the horse[1] that snappeth like a dragon ?' And he made answer and said,

[1] Snapdragon, an English horse.

# THE INDIAN MUTINY

'Verily he could not come, but his heart is with you this day.' And when the young men heard this, they were sorrowful and held their peace.

" And Fawben made a feast for the young men and said, 'Ye have done well this day; come now, eat, drink, and be merry.' And he gave them to eat of bull's flesh, and kid, and savoury meat, and sweet herbs and spices, and provided them with water of the brook Simkin,[1] which is also called dry; and they were exceeding thirsty. And after they had feasted, Fawben took a vessel of silver in his hand and stood up and said, 'Ye have done well this day, and have slain many of the unclean beasts; but there be many that remain to vex the land, so this cup shall be a sign to you, that ye shall not be sparing of your horses until ye have utterly destroyed the soors.' And he gave the vessel of silver to Bedol, as a memorial, for his horse was very swift.

" Then Bedol stood up and said, 'This honour that Fawben hath done me, I am not worthy of it; is he not of the tribe of Brix?' And the young men shouted with one accord, 'Verily, he is chief among the

[1] Hindustani for champagne.

tribe of Brix,' and they danced and made merry before Fawben. And they continued thus for three days, slaying the unclean animals by day, and making merry by night; and whatsoever they desired to eat or to drink, that did Fawben give them; and they were exceeding thirsty. All this did Fawben the collector of taxes do, by reason of his desire to cleanse the land." ("The remainder of the inscription is illegible.")

Another delightful picnic that we had in the cold weather was given by the 37th Regiment, of which we had a wing at Moradabad. The headquarters and right wing were at Bareilly, and the name of the Colonel was John Davis. This picnic lasted for a week, and was at a place called Moondhia Ghat, just within the borders of Nepal, a most beautiful spot on the banks of a fine river—the Surjoo. The camp was pitched on the banks of the river, in a forest of very high trees, and the regimental mess and band of the 37th were present.

In all there were twenty-eight of us, and everyone was provided with a tent and an elephant. The jungles were full of game, including tigers, but it was the wrong time of year for the latter, and we only got one

# THE INDIAN MUTINY

all the time we were out. King George must have shot over the same ground after the last Durbar, but with 600 elephants it does not much matter how thick the jungle is. Still, to get eighteen tigers to his own rifle is a magnificent performance.

Picnics in India are something to think of for the rest of one's life. I shall never forget this one on the borders of Nepal; it was so splendidly done. Neither can I ever forget the kindness of the 37th.

# CHAPTER XX

Simla : We go to Morar, Gwalior : Success of Butterfly : Colonel Gowan : We go home : An experience : Back to India : The favourite beaten : Lord Mayo

AFTERWARDS, when we went to Simla, it was with the view of having another interview with the Commander-in-Chief, and of asking for another appointment. But, as usual, my request failed. I have always found Commanders-in-Chief to be kittle cattle.

Lord Lawrence was still Viceroy, and Government House was the headquarters of croquet. At that time I was considered an expert at the game, and in consequence we were very often at Government House. The Viceroy's appointments were still open to me, but as the examinations were as great an obstacle as ever, I had to depend solely upon the Chief of the Army.

About this time a Major Pierce, who was doing general duty at Moradabad, was appointed second in command of the 33rd N.I. at Morar, Gwalior. Knowing that he would not like it, and my short leave being just up, I returned at once, and asked him if he would exchange with me, and he gladly consented.

It is true that mine was a permanent

# THE INDIAN MUTINY

appointment, though a badly paid one, whilst his was only temporary, the officer holding the appointment having gone home for eighteen months' leave. But I was most anxious to get back to the Native Army. And in the end, after some difficulty, I got what I wanted, though I had to wait for several years.

Gwalior, which was eighty miles south of Agra, was a notoriously hot place. Its fort was on a volcanic rock, rising sheer out of a flat plain and looking right down upon Scindhia's capital, the town of Gwalior. We had put some heavy guns in the fort, which were capable of knocking Scindhia's palace and town into bits in a few minutes. Scindhia, perhaps naturally, thought this a most uncomfortable state of things, and was always trying to persuade the Government to give the fort up to him.

This fort, I may add, was practically impregnable. The road to the fort lay through seven different gateways, all of which were commanded from the high walls. It had never been taken by assault, but was escaladed and surprised by Major Popham very early in the century.

Morar, about three miles away, was our cantonment. All our troops were there, except the small artillery garrison in

## REMINISCENCES OF

Gwalior. The garrison consisted of the Devonshire Regiment, two native infantry regiments, one native cavalry, and two batteries of artillery, so that we had plenty of society.

Besides balls, picnics, croquet, and Badminton, we got up a three days' race meeting. I was one of the stewards, and we were able to persuade Scindhia's Vakeel (Prime Minister) to give us a prize of the value of 500 rupees. Captain W. Strahan, of the Royal Artillery, won the Rajah's cup, and I reserved Butterfly for the other races. I won a race with her on both the first and second days, and on the last day I was twice successful. So Butterfly and I had some reason to congratulate ourselves.

The 33rd were commanded then by Colonel J. Gowan, a most unselfish and thoroughly kind man, who was always trying to do his neighbour a good turn. He was very good to my wife and myself, and gave up the larger part of his bungalow to us. He had had a very bad time of it in the Mutiny, for his regiment had mutinied and killed all the officers they could find. For months he had been compelled to hide in native villages with native friends, who concealed him. These friends used to come and see him at Morar, and he was able to get them well

## THE INDIAN MUTINY

rewarded by the Government for their kindness. The native soldiers loved him, and yet the regiment was in a very bad state. At the time I was extremely puzzled by this, but later on I discovered the reasons.

We stayed with Gowan for eighteen months, until the officer for whom I had been officiating returned from England. Then I found myself stranded and out of employ, and had to do general duty at Meerut. It was now the cold weather of 1870–71, and having completed twenty years' service in June 1869, I was now Major.

General duty, whether at Meerut or anywhere else, means doing nothing. While I was engaged in this arduous work—and I must have been so employed for over a year—I had two duties to perform, one of which was to sit in full uniform, as president of a committee of two, on the retention or otherwise of a worn-out lantern.

Having nothing else to occupy my time, I turned my attention to my racing stable, the training of horses being a special hobby of mine. I bought a Waler mare, Duchess, and an Arab, Silver Mane, and they proved remarkably successful.

In 1871 we took a trip home, and spent a great part of the time in the south of

Ireland, where we made a long stay at St. Anne's Hill, Blarney, which belonged to a Mr. Barter, who was the nephew of my dear old Colonel, Dick Barter, of the 15th Loodiana Sikhs.

While we were staying there a very curious incident happened. On my return one afternoon from fishing, I strolled into the billiard-room and found a friend, who suggested a rubber of whist. To this I agreed, and offered to fetch the cards. Then I went up to our sitting-room, and on opening the door I was surprised to find a party of four sitting round the table engaged in table-turning.

The party consisted of my wife, a Mrs. Glover, Colonel B——, then on leave from Malta, and a young man who was a cripple and at Blarney for the sake of his health. I think this young man was the medium.

As I entered, the Colonel said, "There is a strong spirit wanting to speak to someone in the room." His remark struck me rather forcibly, and I said at once, "May I join you?" I had never been at a séance at any time in my life, but when they had all agreed to let me join them, I sat down between the Colonel and Mrs. Glover, the former of whom was inclined to take command of us all.

# THE INDIAN MUTINY

I said that I should like to ask the name of this spirit, and the table, which was a square one, answered by markedly dipping down to one corner. As each letter was called out by the Colonel, the answer came: "Bannatyne Mac." "That will do," I said, for the Colonel's first remark about a strong spirit had put the idea into my mind that it might be Bannatyne.

As I have mentioned before, Bannatyne Macleod and I were the closest of friends. Our friendship was ideal, and he had always declared that he would communicate with me after death if it was in his power to do so.

I then said, "I should like to ask a question of this spirit." "Tell it me," the Colonel replied, "and I will ask it." "Oh no," I said; "if this is a spirit I need not mention my question to anyone, but shall ask it in my own mind." Then I asked, "What have you to tell me, Bannatyne?" The answer came: "How I love J-a-m-" At this point the Colonel became rather bored, and said, "This is quite commonplace; let us go on to something more interesting." But I begged him to be patient, for I was particularly anxious to hear more. Only my wife and I knew anything about Bannatyne Macleod, but the others knew that my name was James, so I wanted the next letter very badly.

If some one was humbugging, it would evidently be an "e"; but if it really was Bannatyne, an "i" would certainly come; for, being a Highlander, he always called me "Jamie."

An "i" came, to the surprise of the Colonel, but both he and the others seemed to find the proceedings rather dull; when, however, I had assured them that it was anything but dull to me, and that I was satisfied that it really was a message to me from an old friend from another world, they all agreed to continue.

Then I asked in my own mind, "Is it as you and I thought, or is revealed religion necessary to us?" This was to me the most important of all questions, and I awaited the answer with great anxiety. It came out, letter by letter: "Trust to virtue"; and not until the sentence was completed did I find anything at all in it, and then it suddenly flashed on me that this was the most complete answer possible. And indeed it is.

Often have I tried to find a more satisfactory and valuable answer, but I have never succeeded. I have had no more communications from the other world, nor do

## THE INDIAN MUTINY

I require them, for I am absolutely certain that our life is a continuous one, and that only our bodies die.

The autumn of '71 found us back at Meerut and still out of employ; and in the following April we were able to go to Simla, the immense labours of doing general duty not standing in the way!

Lord Mayo was now the Viceroy, and we had made his acquaintance in 1870, and he was now our good friend. In that year I drew the favourite, McGregor, in the Calcutta Derby Lottery, the first prize being £10,000. Up to that time he was the hottest favourite for the Derby ever known, odds of five to two being laid upon him. Lord Mayo had been very interested about this, and at the earliest dawn of the morning after the race, two red-coated chuprassies in succession, one from the Civil Secretary and one from the Military, were at our door with the baneful news that McGregor was fourth and Kingcraft first. Kingcraft was a bad horse, but McGregor had been run on the hard ground at Bath three weeks before, and could not act. The lottery was won by a little milliner, and I am sure that I did not grudge it her. I had hedged a trifle and managed to win about 1800 rupees.

# REMINISCENCES

Lord Mayo now offered me, as had Lord Lawrence, any appointment in his gift, but, as had always happened, I was unable to take advantage of this kindness. My wife was *persona grata* at Government House, and was always getting up theatricals and concerts. In consequence Lord Mayo was very grateful, and could not do enough for us. But all this time the Commander-in-Chief was as obdurate as ever, and the reason why I was always treated in this way was not discovered by me until 1874. And I shall mention it when I come to the events of that year. In '72 I got another acting second in commandship in a native regiment, and curiously enough it was again in Moradabad. Major Armstrong commanded the regiment, and to my surprise I found myself in command of the station. Most officers find this a very trying position, but we got on very well, and when we were inspected by General Sir William Olpherts, he complimented us upon our amiability.

# CHAPTER XXI

*The same old errand : I have my eyes opened : Interview with Lord Napier : Am offered a command : Lord Napier's experience of the Gwalas : We go to Delhi : A parade : I explain my views to my officers*

EIGHTEEN HUNDRED AND SEVENTY-FOUR saw us again in Simla, on the same old errand of seeking a command in the Native Army from the Chief. There was now a new man at the head of the Army, Lord Napier of Magdala. He had been, among many other campaigns, in the China campaign of 1860 and had commanded the Second Division; andI had hopes of him, although I had not been in his division.

To my astonishment I saw in the *Gazette* one day that a man, junior to me, had been given a command of a native regiment. No sooner had I read this than I went straightway to Sir Martin Dillon, the Military Secretary, and asked him the meaning of it. I said, "You have put in a man junior to me, with a record of no particular account, and you have passed me over."

"You," he answered, "why, you are a gambler. There are two black crosses in the Adjutant-General's book against you as a gambler."

This indeed was a revelation, and I knew at last why the various Commanders-in-Chief had passed me over. But I did not intend to listen to this without a strong protest. "Oh," I said, "this is the system of Confidential Reports, the meanest system ever known. By it a man is stabbed in the back, and never has a chance to know anything about the accusation brought against him. I am really obliged to you for letting me know. As it happens I can trace this and can show how little truth there is in it. To think that this has been going on for years, and that I never had the slightest idea of it! I want an interview with the Chief as soon as possible."

"You shall have one to-morrow," he replied, "and I will let you know the time."

"I should like to say, Colonel," I remarked as I went away, "that there are two meanings to the word 'gambler.' First, a man who cheats at cards; secondly, a man who plays for money. Which am I?"

Colonel Dillon was a really good man, and I feel sure that he saw the injustice of this Confidential Report business as well as I did, but he did not mean to commit himself. On the afternoon of the following day I had a private interview with Lord Napier, and made my statement in the following words:

# THE INDIAN MUTINY

" I learn from Colonel Dillon that there are two black marks against me in the Adjutant-General's book for gambling. I want first of all to say that I have been very fond of cards ever since I was seventeen years of age. I have never played for more than I can pay. I have made more friends at the card table than in any other walk of life. No man can say a word in any way against me for playing, no man has ever attempted to do so. I feel sure that I know all about these two crosses. They were put in the book by a man in the Adjutant-General's office. I will mention his name to you if you wish. I was never under his command. He knew nothing about me, but twice in the Simla Club he heard me say aloud, 'I will bet five gold mohurs.' On these slight grounds these crosses were made. The man has retired now, and all these years I have known nothing about this. Had I known I would have taxed him with it, and he would not have been a member of the Simla Club for long. And I maintain, sir, that a man so fond of risk as I have always been, both in purse and person, is much more valuable as a soldier than a man whose chief merit may be that he has never touched a card. Yet, sir, I find myself passed over for a command by ——"

Lord Napier listened to this statement, which amounted almost to a harangue, with the greatest patience, and at the end of it he said that I had put "quite another view upon the matter."

Then I told him—what I had told Colonel Dillon—that there were two meanings to the word "gambler," and he replied that he quite understood, and then added, "There is only one regiment vacant now, and that is the 33rd Native Infantry. I have much pleasure in offering it to you."

I thanked him sincerely, but he interrupted my flow of gratitude. "Don't thank me," he said; "it is the worst regiment in the service. So bad is it, and so badly has it been reported upon for the last eleven years, that the Government are seriously thinking of disbanding it and raising another in its place."

"Well, sir," I returned, "I am nevertheless most sincerely grateful. It is what I want and believe myself to be fit for. I know the regiment. Colonel Gowan commands it, and a better fellow could not be found anywhere."

"The regiment is on the line of march now, and will be at Delhi on January 1. You will meet it there and take command, as Colonel Gowan is going home."

Once more I returned thanks, for this was

# THE INDIAN MUTINY

what I had been wanting for years. I had never commanded a regiment for more than a few days, and the prospect of taking this command gave me the very greatest pleasure.

"Some years ago I officiated as second in command of this regiment for eighteen months," I told Lord Napier, "and if you will allow me I should like to alter the composition of it."

"No," he replied, "that is Imperial business. I cannot do that myself. But why do you want to change it?"

"Because, sir, there are three companies of Gwalas (cowherds) in it."

"What have you to say against them?"

"I don't think that they can stand the racket of war," I replied.

"You mean," Lord Napier replied, "that they are not brave. I will tell you a story. When I was a young man I was very fond of tiger-shooting on foot, and I was out one day in the Bombay Presidency with a native, who was one of your despised Gwalas. It was more or less an open grass jungle, and the man came to me and said, 'Sahib, a tiger has just gone into that piece of grass,' which was only about two acres in extent. So I told him that we would beat through it. We walked right through it, but found no tiger, and I, being a young man, called the native a fool. 'Come back with me, Sahib,' he said, 'and I will show you the tiger,' and to please him I went. He walked up to a clump of grass, and hitting that tiger over the back with his stick, he said, 'Come out of that; don't you know the Sahib is looking for you?' Well, I shot the tiger. You cannot call a man like that a coward, and my opinion is that the Gwalas are about as brave a race of men as I know."

I had no reply ready at that time, but I have since found out the truth of the matter. The Gwalas as a race are well acquainted with tigers from their earliest youth, when as little boys they go out with the herds. They know that the tiger is not in the least interested in them, but that if he wants anything his choice will fall upon a fat cow. The boy, even if he is only four or five years old, will go and take up his place behind the big bull of the herd and is never hurt. But when there is a man-eating tiger about, an old chap with bad teeth who cannot manage a big cow, there is nobody more afraid than a Gwala. Shortly afterwards the battle of Maiwand showed that my opinion of the Gwalas was not incorrect.

The result, then, of my visit to Lord Napier was that we packed up all our goods

# THE INDIAN MUTINY

and chattels at Moradabad, and went to Delhi to meet the regiment on January 1. Gowan was going home to England immediately, and I insisted upon the regiment giving him a dinner. This farewell festivity did not seem to have been suggested by any one, although Gowan was such an exceedingly good sort.

He did not leave until the morning of the 3rd, and I would not assume power until he left. Then I ordered a parade. I never saw anything in my life like this exhibition; it was so utterly bad that I could not stand it for more than a few minutes, and at the end of that time I sounded the "Halt" and "Officers fall out," and they all came up and saluted.

"Gentlemen," I said to them, "the Chief told me that this regiment was in a bad state. It is in such a frightful state that I have never seen anything to approach it. It is so bad that I shall not have another parade for six weeks."

Then the Adjutant sidled up to me and whispered, "But, sir, if we are so bad, how shall we get any better if you do not have parades?"

"Make your mind easy," I said, "you cannot possibly be worse." I dismissed the regiment, and all the officers went to the mess, where a sort of official meeting was held. Each officer came up to me, in his turn, and the Adjutant was the first to come. "Sir," he said, "here are the books of the Adjutant's office. Will you take them over? Colonel Gowan always looked after them."

Then the Quartermaster came up. "Here are the books of the Quartermaster's office," he said; "Colonel Gowan kept them, and I hope you will do the same. I think they are correct up to date."

After this the band accounts were produced, and I was begged to follow Colonel Gowan's example and take them. Then another officer brought forward the mess books, and assured me that Colonel Gowan had always presided over the mess, and that he hoped I would do the same.

I waited until they had all done, and then I addressed them. "Gentlemen, you are all very much mistaken in me," I began, "for I am a very lazy man. You seem to think that I have come here to do all the work of the regiment, but nothing is further from my intention. I am not going to do the work; I have come here to see you do it. There is a very good racquet-court here, I am glad to say, and I am very fond of racquets, and hope very often to play with you. You, Captain S——," I continued, "will be

## THE INDIAN MUTINY

Adjutant. I really meant that I do not intend to have a parade for six weeks, so that your duties for the present will not be arduous. I shall be able later on to explain my views to you. You, Lieutenant B——, will be Quartermaster, and I shall have something to say about the dress of the regiment, which I think wants some alteration. I mean to put the men into gaiters, for at present, with their ammunition-boots, their legs look like mop-sticks in buckets. You, Major R——, will be president of the band. It seems to be very good, but I am not qualified to take charge of a band. I hope you are. You, Captain M——, will, I am sure, have great pleasure in taking charge of the mess. I am very pleased to hear that you are a first-class French *chef*, for I am very fond of a good dinner."

The reasons, to my mind, for the regiment having fallen into this state were, firstly, that Colonel Gowan liked to do everything himself, and consequently he never gave any officer a chance of responsibility, but he would give all the officers as much leave as they wanted. Secondly—and I had seen this before in many other regiments, notably in the one in which I had acted as second in command at Barrackpore—the men had been drilled and drilled and drilled, and the punishment for not doing well had been more drill. I knew something about the fighting classes of India, and was well aware that they are keen upon drill. But, of course, if you are everlastingly drilling, any race in the world will get sick and tired of it.

Well, my officers at first did not believe in me. They thought this idea of no drill was absolutely fatal, and also, naturally, they were all more or less disappointed in losing a step; for I was an outsider, and, in consequence, there was no promotion. And, as regards the men, those who knew me possibly liked me more or less; but, compared with Colonel Gowan, who had been the friend of natives all his life, and who had obtained land and honours for those who had helped him during the Mutiny, I could not expect to stand high.

At the end of six weeks I had a parade, but it was quite unlike anything they had ever seen before, for there was no left-wheel into line or forming column. The moment they came on parade I took them in hand without going through any formula, and gave them five minutes of manœuvres at the double; and they were back in their lines before they knew where they were.

We were within the walls of a large and

# THE INDIAN MUTINY

more or less fanatical city. Disturbances with the inhabitants were expected, and before I had held the command for a fortnight we had a small one. Then I had a talk with the native officers, and plainly spoke my mind to them. I suppose that this had some effect, for we never had another disturbance of any sort or kind; and during the five years of my command I never had more than one court-martial a year, which must, I should think, be nearly a record.

# CHAPTER XXII

Improvement of the regiment : An inspection : Praise and explanations : A good dinner : Snakes : Sham fights : The Prince of Wales's visit : A new game of tennis : Ulwar : A magnificent picnic

WE were, so we heard, to be inspected, in the second week of April of this year, by General Sir William Payn, who was commanding the division. As time went on I had longer and longer parades, and I found that the men were coming to hand very well, and that both officers and men were much pleased by the alteration of the hours of parades. Previously it had always been the custom to have parade at phenomenally early hours. This I found was detested by both officers and men alike, and as to feeling the effects of the sun I discovered that everybody was quite willing to parade at 9 or 10 A.M., instead of 4 in the early morning. The men especially liked this alteration.

When April came my officers were very uneasy about the few parades which I had held, and the Adjutant came and begged me to have a few parades in the afternoon as the bayonet exercise was not smartly done. "My good fellow," I said, "I am

# THE INDIAN MUTINY

not going to have a single extra parade for any general that was ever born. You and I know more about this regiment than anybody else does. Do you imagine that I can't put this through?"

The much dreaded General came, and gave us two good hours of first-class drill. Then he sounded "Officers fall out," and we all went up and saluted.

"Harris," he said to me, "do you know what I am going to say of your regiment?"

"No, sir," I replied, "but I hope it is nothing very bad."

"I am going to say that it is the best regiment in my division. There is not a regiment in the division, European or native, that drills like it. Now," he continued, "everyone knows the record of this regiment. For the last eleven years I know that it has been reported upon as the worst in the service, and now I find it the best. What is the meaning of it?"

"I do not want to tell you, sir," was my reply.

"Why?"

"Because, sir, I have broken most of the regulations of the service, and I do not want to get into trouble."

"Trouble!" he exclaimed, "there will

be no trouble when I see a regiment drilled like this."

"Then," I said, "if you will keep me clear of anything of the sort, I shall be glad to tell you. I have heard, sir, that in your younger days you had a racing stable. I have also had one for the last fifteen years. You know, sir, that if you gallop a horse for two miles every day on the same course and at the same pace, you ultimately make him so slow that you can kick your hat along as fast as he can gallop."

"Oh," he said, "you mean that the men were stale."

"Stale and more than stale. I never saw anything like it for staleness, and I guessed it must be that. All these races that enlist are really fond of drill, but they had been given too much of it."

"What are the regimental institutions like?"

"They are, I think, very good. Colonel Gowan left them," I added, "in excellent order, and they are at least as good now as when I took them over, and the mess is first-rate. You are coming to dine with us to-night, sir, and you are going to have the best dinner you have seen in India."

"Then it is too expensive for the young hands," he told me.

# THE INDIAN MUTINY

"What do you think, sir, that an officer's messing should come to a day?"

"I should not object if it was four rupees."

"We do it for 2 rupees 8 annas. You dined, sir, with the regiment in the Fort last night. They are all very good fellows, but I am glad to see that you have survived their dinner!"

Then he laughed and said, "Yes, I survived it all right. There must be something behind all this, something more than I have been told, for you to have got the regiment into this state."

"The fact is," I replied, "that Colonel Gowan always liked to do everything himself. He did not give any of his officers any responsibility at all, but I have been going on quite different lines. Each officer does his own work in this regiment. I have nothing to do but to see that the work is done. It is the easiest thing in the world, and I find that it is appreciated by everyone. The whole of my work is done in under ten minutes with a bit of paper and a pencil."

We had a very nice messhouse on the walls, overlooking the Jumna, and our fine old tables of Bombay blackwood were so beautifully polished that we merely put two slips over them. The General sat on my right at dinner, and before we had got half through the meal he said, " Harris, you are right. I have never seen a dinner like it in India. But I don't understand it."

" Well, sir," I replied, " that man, Major M——, sitting at the end of the table, is the best French cook in India. He is a student of cookery, and he does not mind taking any amount of trouble. He will sit, as I am sure he has been doing this very afternoon, in an armchair on the verandah, drinking shandy-gaff, with five different natives cooking separate dishes. Then my wife is also a most excellent English cook. We entertain a good deal, and we have established a kind of friendly rivalry between the two styles. Nearly everyone in this station wants to be an honorary member of our mess, and as we sit down thirty-two to dinner every night it is easy to be more or less economical. The only extras we have to-night are the pomfret, and the oysters from Bombay."

For the first time in twelve years the regiment was reported upon in terms of the highest praise, and next year another General Officer reported in the same manner. But in the third year of my command the authorities at Simla, having, I think, heard of our good dinners, sent a special man to

# THE INDIAN MUTINY

inspect, who evidently had orders not to accept our hospitality, for he would not dine nor lunch, nor even have a glass of sherry in our mess, and he lived at the dāk bungalow. He had been given to understand that Colonel Harris (for by this time I was Colonel) had a way of humbugging Generals by the quality of his entertainments.

We had some changes in the regiment, for the Adjutant died suddenly of aneurism, and B—— took his place. To my mind he was not exactly fitted for the post. He was a born naturalist, and knew more about snakes than anyone I have ever met.

One morning two of my officers came to see me, and said, "I wish, sir, you would speak to B——. He, as you know, lives quite close to the messhouse, and yesterday there was a large snake crawling across the messroom, and to-day there was another. He has got about forty living snakes under his bed. You know, sir, he is rather careless, and we don't altogether like it."

"All right; send B—— to me," I told them, and when he had come I asked him to explain the fact that snakes were crawling around the messroom.

"They are quite harmless, sir," he assured me. "I have got over forty of them in my room, and yesterday I caught the finest black cobra I have seen."

"How do you catch them?" I asked.

"In my hand, sir. You know all those aloe hedges close by the musketry range; they are full of snakes. I am constantly on the range and in uniform, and in these tall boots no snake can hurt me. When I see a snake I go over and try to get my foot right across it, so that it goes in the hollow between the heel and the ball of my foot. But directly it turns to bite me it bites my boot, and I catch it round the neck with my left hand. With my pocket-handkerchief in my right hand I make him open his mouth. Then I make a little snood, and put it over first one fang and then the other, and pull out both of them. After that they are perfectly harmless."

"I will come and see your snakes," I told him, and when we had reached his bungalow, I found, sure enough, that under his bed and, indeed, all about the room were little earthenware pots with a loose saucer top.

"Now, sir," he said, "I will show you the finest black cobra de capello you probably have ever seen."

He took off the saucer of one of these pots and then tapped the side, and up sprang a snake. He caught it round the neck

## THE INDIAN MUTINY

with his left hand and said, "Now, sir, I will show you how I take out the fangs of snakes."

Having produced his little snood, he opened the mouth of the snake with his left hand and pulled out the fang and also about three drops of a fine amber fluid, which was more than enough to kill every officer in my regiment.

"I knew you were always a careless chap," I told him, "but now I know that you have been risking the lives of all your brother officers. All these snakes must go. You may keep snakes bottled in spirits, but if you want to keep live snakes, you will keep them out of cantonments. I will not have a single one of them in cantonments. And I really think," I continued, "that you are more fitted for the Forest Department than for an adjutancy of any regiment. I believe I can help you in that way, and, if you like, I will write a letter to the head of that department, who is a personal friend of mine, and suggest that you would be a very valuable man for him. Will that suit you?"

"I should like nothing better," he informed me, and within two months it was all arranged. He went to the Forest Department, where he remained during the remainder of his service in India, and became more or less famous as an entomologist. James Graves Kelly (who had become Quartermaster when Stekelin died) now became Adjutant, and I could not have had a better man. Kelly was the man who afterwards relieved Chitral and became A.D.C. to the Queen.

Delhi was a very stirring place in the years following 1875. The great camp of exercise, the visit of the Prince of Wales, and the first Imperial Durbar all came off while we were in Delhi.

The first of these consisted of a series of sham fights on an enormous scale. The different forces started, as a rule, about forty miles apart, and generally they represented a large force endeavouring to enter Delhi, and a much smaller force defending the approaches to it.

It was a very great advantage to me to have an intimate knowledge of the country. This knowledge I had picked up while pig-sticking with the Delhi Tent Club, of which I was President, and my experiences during the Mutiny were also of some value. I remember on one occasion, when I was commanding the smaller force retreating on Delhi, that I led the "enemy" into such an ambuscade that the General, coming up at the moment

# THE INDIAN MUTINY

with two umpires, sounded the "Cease fire," and said, "Gentlemen, you can all go home; Harris has killed the lot of you."

The visit of the Prince of Wales does not recall to my mind anything particularly remarkable, excepting that it was a series of very fine reviews. On the other hand, the Imperial assemblage in the following year was a sight that I can never forget. I do not believe that even the last Durbar can have surpassed it, for I think that the absence of elephants must have deprived it of some of its attractiveness.

On the second day the Rajah and potentates of all sorts, with their respective bodyguards, passed in review before Lord Lytton. Some of these were most amusing, and all of them were interesting. The Ranee of Tanjore's elephants were quite a feature, as they were all painted sky-blue, with pink faces and magnificent gold howdahs.

Cashmere had a bodyguard of some 50 cavalry, wearing the enormous brass helmets of Cuirassiers of the Guard in Napoleon's time. But the most amusing of all, in my opinion, was the Rajah of Jheend's bodyguard. He had taken a great fancy to our Highlanders, and he had dressed his bodyguard to imitate them. They wore kilts, and he had their brown legs painted pink. The escorts of the various Rajputana chiefs were, perhaps, the most beautifully got up.

In the last Durbar there does not seem to have been any similar march past.

During all this time we were living in our comfortable house on the walls of Delhi, and I had spent some of my leisure hours inventing a new game of tennis within walls, and had built a court in my own compound. This game I considered to be most attractive, and the most remarkable thing about it was that the better you played the longer was the rally. This was the more surprising as the net was only two feet six inches high.

It was my object to get the best racquet and tennis players in India to stay with me, and in this I was very successful. To give an idea of the length of the rally, I was sitting outside the court one day, and it struck me that the marker had called "Played" a great number of times. So I began to count, and after this I counted "Played" 71 times. Now, the men playing were two really good men of the Artillery, who had both played in their regimental matches against the Engineers.

Twenty-two courts that I know of were built on the lines of mine by various messes or clubs. But most, if not all, of these

# THE INDIAN MUTINY

did not succeed; some failed because the players did not get the balls, the racquets, and the floor to fit; and others failed because people considered that they could improve upon the original design. The 15th Hussars built a more expensive court, with higher walls, and the corners closed in all round. But you can never possibly take a tennis ball out of a closed corner. The ends of the sides of my court were open; to close them in meant the complete destruction of the game.

Thousands of games of tennis were played in this court of mine, and by the best players in India; and, though many prejudices had to be overcome, I do not remember anyone who did not own that it was a really good game. Any unbiased lover of games must admit that a game between two very skilful lawn-tennis players in which there were constantly rallies of a hundred must be good. Look at lawn tennis of the present day. To my mind it is more or less spoilt as a game by the extraordinary skill of the players. And racquets seem to me to be in much the same case. I am thinking not only of those who look on at games, but also of those who play them.

I would here mention that the racquets which we used were rough-strung, and the balls covered with wash-leather.

I have before mentioned that India is the place of all places for picnics. In England the majority of people, when they are asked to a picnic, begin to search for an excuse or a previous engagement, but in India a picnic is a thing to go to. During the cold weather I received a letter from an old friend, Tommy Cadell, who had been subaltern a little junior to me in the old 2nd European Bengal Fusiliers; he was with me in the attack the enemy made on us at the Flagstaff picket on June 12, 1857, for his share in which I recommended him for the V.C., which he got.

This letter was written from Ulwar, a native State some 70 or 80 miles south from Delhi. And it appeared that Tommy was resident at the court of Ulwar, and that Ulwar had just come or was just coming of age, and in consequence proposed to give the European Sahibs a great picnic.

Invitations were enclosed to the effect that His Highness requested the pleasure of my wife's and my company, with as many of my friends as I liked to bring to the picnic at Ulwar. The date was early in January, and we were asked to stay for three days. Special trains each way, and every other imaginable convenience, were to be provided.

# THE INDIAN MUTINY

The line to Ulwar was a narrow gauge, and had not long been opened. Having got leave from the officer commanding the station for the officers and myself, we left Delhi just before midnight by the special train. We were a party of nine—my wife, a young niece out from England, myself, and six of my fellows; various other members of the community made up the train party to between thirty and forty. There was also a contingent from Agra and other stations, but they went by other routes. I think that altogether there were nearly ninety guests.

Having arrived at Ulwar at 8 A.M. on the following morning, we were met at the railway station by the Rajah's Vakeel (Prime Minister). Notebook in hand and bowing profoundly, he addressed me, "You are Colonel Harris, I think?" and I replied with a bow. "How many is your party?" and I told him that there were nine of us. Then having, as it were, entered us in his notebook, he said, "I propose to give you one four-in-hand, three landaus, three dog-carts or buggies, and as many riding horses as you please. Will that do?" I responded that I thought it would "do" splendidly. "They are in waiting here," he continued, "but if you would prefer elephants they are here also." Whereupon

I said, "There is only one thing. I have been teaching my niece to ride, and I should like to choose her horse." "Certainly, certainly," he said, "you choose any you like; we have 500 in the stables."

This word "stables" causes me furiously to think. I went to inspect these stables during the afternoon, so that I might choose a really good horse for my niece. And there I found a management which might well make many Englishmen blush, even at the present day. Each horse was secured by head ropes and one heel rope, and he stood on his own platform of nine or ten inches of dry earth. At the end of each row of stables was a platform of tiles, with flues under it. On this any earth that had become damp was thrown and spread about so that it might dry. Two or three boys were employed in every line of stables. Every particle of wet earth was at once removed, and either thrown on to the flue or carried away.

Contrast this with our own stables, frequently of cobble-stones, the best of them of enamelled tiles, with straw on the top and smelling strongly of ammonia. In these stables there was no smell whatever. There each horse pawed his mattress until he got it to suit him, and then he lay on what was

## THE INDIAN MUTINY

—to him—practically a feather bed. Even in our best racing stables a horse but rarely lies down, for straw on the top of either enamelled tile or cobble-stones is not comfortable enough to induce him to do so. The result of this system of Ulwar's was that nearly every horse was lying down. I have been a horse master for many years, and I have been over many of the best stables in England, and also over many tramway and omnibus stables, and in these last I have seen a vast amount of unintentional cruelty to horses. I think that Ulwar's stables were a pattern to the world.

It was, perhaps, a mile from the station to our camp, which was in a semicircle on good turf, round a large projecting bow-windowed hall of the palace. In this we all had our meals to the sound of bugles. The tents were very large and comfortable, the meals were magnificent, and, if you wished, you could swim in champagne from breakfast until dinner.

On the afternoon of the first day those who felt inclined rode out to see the Rajah's cheetahs hunt the antelopes of the country. These cheetahs were on the ordinary agricultural carts of the country. The antelopes fed in herds among the growing crops. When the carts got within a hundred yards of a herd the spectacles, made of hide, were taken off one of the cheetahs, and he stood quite free upon the cart. If he thought that he was within five springs he immediately dashed for the herd, and if he could pounce on an antelope in these five springs he got it; if he failed he sulked and was troublesome. But as a rule he seemed to be able to secure his prey. There was also pig-sticking for some of us, and in the evening an excellent dinner, a capital hall for dancing, and a splendid band.

On the next day the great hunt took place. My niece had tried the horse which I had chosen for her, and was quite pleased with it; but I chose an elephant for my mount, and was accompanied by a friend, a judge from Agra.

The hunt was a drag, and a considerable field of nearly thirty mounted men started. Through Ulwar, right across the whole of India to the east coast, somewhere in Orissa, runs the great Customs Hedge. This hedge is necessary because of the duties on salt, which is a Government monopoly in India. It is constantly patrolled, and has gates wherever a road goes through it. It is made entirely of sprays of thorns, and is from eight to ten feet high and very broad. After about half an hour's galloping the

# THE INDIAN MUTINY

field came to this hedge, and most of them charged it, my niece and all my young fellows being among the number. My niece got well over, but all the rest of them got into the thorns. I, on the elephant, was on the flank with my friend from Agra, and we enjoyed this incident very much; for if it was rather painful to take part in, it was certainly most amusing to watch.

Most of the third day was devoted to shooting alligators, which abounded in a large lake close to us. There was an island in this lake, and there seemed to be about a dozen alligators upon it at all times of the day.

The country swarmed with peacocks, but with them, of course, we did not interfere, for in a Hindoo State they are sacred. Many of us, however, got good bags of partridges and small game. An exhibition of fireworks took place every night, and this was seen to the greatest advantage, as most of the Palace was built round an enormous tank. The Rajah always favoured us with his company at dinner, and, altogether, his hospitality was as lavish as it is memorable.

## CHAPTER XXIII

Native history : Exploration : Buried treasure : A company is formed : Difficulties with the directors : Farewell

DELHI was always a most interesting place to me, and I have always felt the charm of native history. My first station with my old regiment had been Agra, and there I had lived for two years with Bannatyne Macleod, who had native history at his fingers' ends.

I had read much of the Great Moguls: of Shah Jehan, who built the Taj; of Akbar the Great, who lies buried at Secundra, only five miles from the Taj. Futtehpore Sikri, Deig, Bhurtpore, I knew, though these were only side interests; and here was I, stationed for years in Delhi, the home of this ruling race.

I made a practice of exploring the seven ruined cities of Old Delhi. Every Sunday throughout the cold weather we (that is, most of my officers and myself, with anyone else who liked to join us) started off to explore some old tomb, or perhaps some bit of what looked like fortification, or, maybe, we tried to localise some fragment of ancient history. Humayon's tomb, Nizam-o-deen, Sufder Jung, The Kootub, Toglukhabad,

## THE INDIAN MUTINY

and many others unknown to fame, were explored by us. In fact, all the country west of the Jumna was familiar to me.

I had many native friends, and was constantly hearing stories from them of low-caste men—who were supposed to make their living by digging bricks out of the ruins and selling them to builders in modern Delhi—finding treasure in the shape of gold mohurs, and disappearing from the ken of men. I, of course, knew that there were no banks in the country, and that everyone who had any money always buried it. So it became more or less of a certainty in my mind that these miles of ruins contained an immense quantity of treasure. And I think that this treasure is still to be found, not only in Delhi and its neighbourhood, but also in many other parts of India known to me.

I took a trip to Lahore, and saw the head of the Government. I stated my views candidly to him, and asked for a concession of the right to dig for treasure in Government lands; furthermore I stated that these old ruined cities were worth practically nothing, as only a few goats grazed over them.

"Will you agree," he asked, "to leave the land fit for agriculture?"

"Certainly," was my reply.

"And will you also pay five per cent. to the Government of all treasure found?" And again I assured him that I would, for these were good terms and I accepted them gladly. I was back at Delhi inside forty-eight hours, with my concession duly signed.

I had had some experience in limited liability companies, and I drew up a prospectus for "The Delhi Ancient Treasure Company, Ltd.," with a capital of 100,000 rupees in 20,000 shares of five rupees each. The expenditure of forming the company amounted to only 300 rupees, and I made over all my rights to the company, in return for which I allotted myself 300 shares fully paid. This was not exactly an avaricious proceeding, as I think will generally be admitted. Then I picked out five of my native friends and made them directors, and I chose a very good fellow, a European pleader in the Courts, to be solicitor and secretary to the company.

I could not be a director myself, as the regulations of the service did not allow an officer to be director of any company. This was unfortunate, but it could not be helped. The shares were readily subscribed, and I myself took a thousand ordinary shares. In

## THE INDIAN MUTINY

a few days the five-rupee share was worth twenty rupees, and every day the shares continued to advance in price.

Then I said, "We will now dig." I drew a straight line a hundred yards long, and started digging in a westerly direction. At a depth of 21 feet we came to water, below which I felt sure that we should find nothing. Earth-work was extraordinarily cheap. All stones, bricks, &c., were buried behind us as we advanced, and covered over with earth. We made very rapid progress.

On the second day some coolies dug the front face too deeply, and the earth fell on them and one coolie was killed. This sent the shares up to 55 rupees, the natives saying that we must be very near the treasure, as the devils guarding it had killed a man. I thought that this was a good opportunity to sell some of my thousand ordinary shares.

During the following day the directors came to me in a body and said, "Sahib, the shares are now worth 55 rupees, and we must not spend the money or the shares will go down."

"But we are scarcely spending anything. See what a lot of ground we have opened up, and altogether we have not spent 1500 rupees," I replied.

"Yes, yes," they agreed, "but we must

not spend the money or the shares will go down."

"But," I protested, "we *must* spend the money, or how can we find the treasure?"

I, however, could do nothing with them, for whatever I said to them, their answer was invariably the same.

"Well," I said at last, "you are the directors and can do what you like. But you must remember that this company was formed for the purpose of digging for treasure."

Subsequently I had several interviews, but always with no result. So, finding that I could not persuade them to dig, I sold all of my remaining ordinary shares.

"If you won't spend money, what will you do?" I asked them.

"We are going to dig by the advice of astrologers," they replied.

"And who is your principal astrologer?"

In answer to this question I was told that the coachman of the Commissioner Sahib was a first-rate astrologer, and that they were going to dig by his advice. He knew of a place, so I was told, where they should dig on the thirteenth day of the dark half of the month. They were to kill a white cock, and to sprinkle his blood on all the four corners of the place at midnight, and the

## THE INDIAN MUTINY

devils would then be unable to remove the treasure. The astrologer was to be paid thirty rupees. Astrology seemed to be cheap, but it was also, I must add, entirely unsuccessful.

The directors had their own way and found nothing, but the shares still remained in the neighbourhood of 55.

Soon afterwards I brought forward a scheme and said to them: "You all know the old palace of Ferozeshah, with the pillar of Asoka in the middle. I have here a contractor who has measured the ground, and will contract to dig the whole down to the water for 75,000 rupees. It contains, as you know, a considerable quantity of black marble slabs, and everything we find, less five per cent., will be the property of the company. If you directors will see the contractor, you will doubtless be able to make a better bargain with him than I can. Some of you, I am sure, know a great deal about the history of Ferozeshah's times, and also of the tradition of the twenty-three crores of rupees (£23,000,000) he had in that place. You are always telling me the shares will go down if we spend money. I should like you to think of what they will go up to if we find even a thousand gold mohurs."

But I might as well have saved my exertions and breath, for nothing that I could say would move them. By this time they knew that as directors the power was completely in their hands, and they intended to use it as they—and not as I—wished.

As a last move, I called a general meeting of the company and addressed it to this effect:

"This company, as the prospectus shows, was founded for the express purpose of digging for ancient treasure. These intentions your directors refuse to carry out. We have ample funds, but you will not use them. Altogether, you have not spent 2000 rupees in digging, and our capital is 100,000. I give you warning that if in a month's time you still refuse to carry out the intentions of the prospectus, I shall file a petition to the Government to wind up the company."

This I eventually had to do, and the company was wound up. I sold the few shares I still had left and took sick leave to England. I was very much disgusted, for I thought then, and still think, that we wasted a most excellent opportunity. Nor is Delhi the only likely place, but it had this peculiarity, that at least once

## THE INDIAN MUTINY

in its history it had 150,000 inhabitants killed in three days. Under such circumstances many traces of treasure must have disappeared.

Then think also of how the Mahrattas and the Pindarees swept the country for years with their hordes of cavalry. Their methods were simple. If a man was fat, which in India always means rich, he was naturally suspected of having buried treasure. The usual treatment accorded him was to cut off his upper eyelids, and then push his head into a horse's nose-bag which contained plenty of red pepper.

Were we English to leave India and allow the Indians to rule the country, as many people, mostly, however, Bengalees, wish, some of these delightful practices would doubtless recur. It is well that the Bengalee Baboo should remember that there are more fat and rich people in Bengal than in any other part of India.

And now, having ventured to recount some of the incidents in the earlier—and more adventurous—part of my life, I will end with a hope that I have not hurt the feelings or wounded the sensibilities of any of my readers, and with the assurance that nothing has been set down in malice.

# REMINISCENCES

Should it happen, however, that I am held to have been more outspoken than most writers, I can only say with David Harum, "If I have said anything I am sorry for, I am willing to be forgiven."

Most of my friends have passed on to the Great Beyond. But if I have given a little amusement to those who remain by chronicling these events of my life and by calling up pleasant memories of bygone days, I am satisfied.

To all my old Mutiny comrades, and to all friends, old and new, I would say "Good-bye" and "Au revoir."

JIM HARRIS

IMPERIAL HOTEL, BARNSTAPLE
*April* 19, 1912

BALLANTYNE & COMPANY LTD
TAVISTOCK STREET COVENT GARDEN
LONDON

www.ingramcontent.com/pod-product-compliance
Lightning Source LLC
Chambersburg PA
CBHW050142170426
43197CB00011B/1927